PRENTICE HALL
LITERATURE

Reader's
COMPANION
Adapted Version

The American Experience

PEARSON
Prentice Hall

Upper Saddle River, New Jersey
Needham, Massachusetts

ISBN 0-13-180294-1

6 7 8 9 10   09 08 07 06 05

Acknowledgments

Grateful acknowledgment is made to the following for permission to reprint copyrighted material:

Sandra Dijkstra Literary Agency for Amy Tan
From "Mother Tongue" by Amy Tan. Copyright © 1989 by Amy Tan. First appeared in *Threepenny Review*.

Rita Dove
Rita Dove, "For the Love of Books," first published as part of the *Introduction To Selected Poems*, Pantheon Books/Vintage Books, © 1993 by Rita Dove.

Farrar, Straus & Giroux, Inc.
From "The First Seven Years" from *The Magic Barrel* by Bernard Malamud. Copyright © 1950, 1958 and copyright renewed © 1977, 1986 by Bernard Malamud.

Harcourt Brace & Company
From "A Worn Path" from *A Curtain Of Green And Other Stories*, copyright 1941 and renewed 1969 by Eudora Welty. From "Everyday Use" from *In Love & Trouble: Stories Of Black Women*, copyright © 1973 by Alice Walker.

W. W. Norton & Company, Inc.
From "Civil Disobedience" reprinted from *Walden And Civil Disobedience* by Henry David Thoreau, edited by Owen Thomas. Copyright ©1966 by W. W. Norton & Company, Inc.

Scribner, a division of Simon & Schuster, Inc.
From "The Far and the Near" from *Death To Morning* by Thomas Wolfe. Copyright 1935 by Charles Scribner's Sons; copyright renewed © 1963 by Paul Gitlin. From "In Another Country" from MEN WITHOUT WOMEN by Ernest Hemingway. Copyright 1927 by Charles Scribner's Sons. Copyright renewed 1955 by Ernest Hemingway.

Sterling Lord Literistic, Inc.
From "The Crisis, Number 1" by Thomas Paine from *Citizen Tom Paine*. Copyright by Howard Fast.

Syracuse University Press
From "The Iroquois Constitution" from *Parker On The Iroquois: Iroquois Uses Of Maize And Other Food Plants; The Code Of Handsome Lake; The Seneca Prophet; The Constitution Of The Five Nations* by Arthur C. Parker, edited by William N. Fenton (Syracuse University Press, Syracuse, NY, 1981).

USA Today
"Lawyers Leave Poor Behind" from *USA Today* (September 25, 2000). Copyright © 2000 by *USA Today*.

Viking Penguin, Inc., A Division of Penguin Goup (USA) Inc.
"On Social Plays" copyright © 1955, 1978 by Arthur Miller, from *The Theater Essays of Arthur Miller* by Arthur Miller, edited by Robert A. Martin. From "The Turtle (Chapter 3)" from *The Grapes Of Wrath* by John Steinbeck, copyright 1939, renewed © 1967 by John Steinbeck.

Robert N. Wiener
"Pro Bono Work Still Valued" by Robert N. Weiner from *USA Today* (September 25, 2000). Copyright © 2000 by Robert N. Weiner.

Note: Every effort has been made to locate the copyright owner of material reprinted in this book. Omissions brought to our attention will be corrected in subsequent editions.

Contents

Part 2: Reading Informational Materials **205**

Part 1

Selection Adaptations With Excerpts of Authentic Text

Part 1 will guide and support you as you interact with selections from *Prentice Hall Literature: Timeless Voices, Timeless Themes*. Part 1 provides summaries of literature selections with passages from the selection.

- Begin with the Preview page in the *Reader's Companion Adapted Version*. Use the written and visual summaries to preview the selections before you read.

- Then study the Prepare to Read page. This page introduces skills that you will apply as you read selections in the *Reader's Companion Adapted Version*.

- Now read the selection in the *Reader's Companion Adapted Version*.

- Respond to all the questions along the sides as you read. They will guide you in understanding the selection and in applying the skills. Write in the *Reader's Companion Adapted Version*—really! Circle things that interest you. Underline things that puzzle you. Number ideas or events to help you keep track of them. Look for the **Mark the Text** logo for help with active reading.

- Use the Review and Assess questions at the end of each selection to review what you have read and to check your understanding.

- Finally, do the Writing or the Speaking and Listening activity to extend your understanding and practice your skills.

Interacting With the Text

As you read, use the information and notes to guide you in interacting with the selection. The examples on these pages show you how to use the notes as a companion when you read. They will guide you in applying reading and literary skills and in thinking about the selections. When you read other texts, you can practice the thinking skills and strategies found here.

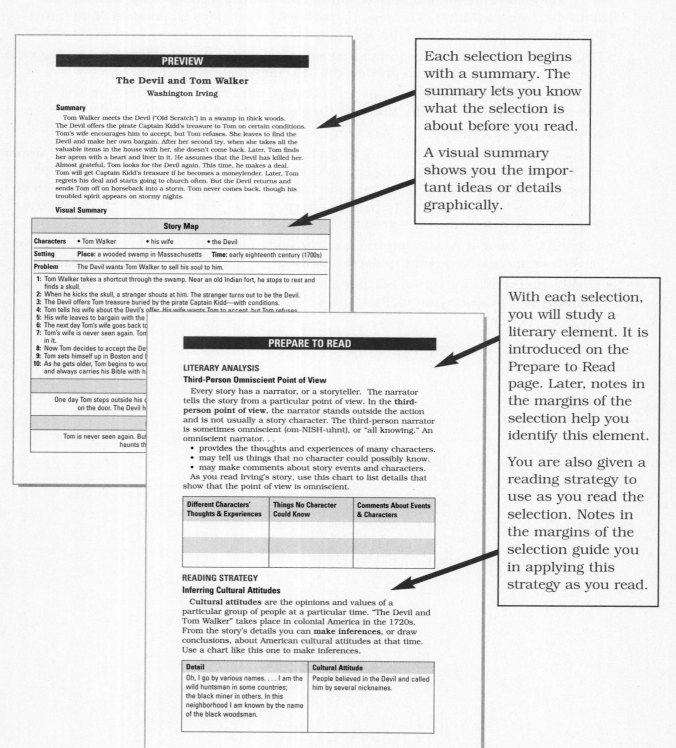

PREVIEW

The Devil and Tom Walker
Washington Irving

Summary

Tom Walker meets the Devil ("Old Scratch") in a swamp in thick woods. The Devil offers the pirate Captain Kidd's treasure to Tom on certain conditions. Tom's wife encourages him to accept, but Tom refuses. She leaves to find the Devil and make her own bargain. After her second try, when she takes all the valuable items in the house with her, she doesn't come back. Later, Tom finds her apron with a heart and liver in it. He assumes that the Devil has killed her. Almost grateful, Tom looks for the Devil again. This time, he makes a deal. Tom will get Captain Kidd's treasure if he becomes a moneylender. Later, Tom regrets his deal and starts going to church often. But the Devil returns and sends Tom off on horseback into a storm. Tom never comes back, though his troubled spirit appears on stormy nights.

Visual Summary

Story Map		
Characters	• Tom Walker • his wife • the Devil	
Setting	**Place:** a wooded swamp in Massachusetts **Time:** early eighteenth century (1700s)	
Problem	The Devil wants Tom Walker to sell his soul to him.	

1: Tom Walker takes a shortcut through the swamp. Near an old Indian fort, he stops to rest and finds a skull.
2: When he kicks the skull, a stranger shouts at him. The stranger turns out to be the Devil.
3: The Devil offers Tom treasure buried by the pirate Captain Kidd—with conditions.
4: Tom tells his wife about the Devil's offer. His wife wants Tom to accept, but Tom refuses.
5: His wife leaves to bargain with the
6: The next day Tom's wife goes back to
7: Tom's wife is never seen again. Tom in it.
8: Now Tom decides to accept the De
9: Tom sets himself up in Boston and
10: As he gets older, Tom begins to wor and always carries his Bible with hi

One day Tom steps outside his on the door. The Devil h

Tom is never seen again. But haunts th

Each selection begins with a summary. The summary lets you know what the selection is about before you read.

A visual summary shows you the important ideas or details graphically.

PREPARE TO READ

LITERARY ANALYSIS
Third-Person Omniscient Point of View

Every story has a narrator, or a storyteller. The narrator tells the story from a particular point of view. In the **third-person point of view**, the narrator stands outside the action and is not usually a story character. The third-person narrator is sometimes omniscient (om-NISH-uhnt), or "all knowing." An omniscient narrator. . .

• provides the thoughts and experiences of many characters.
• may tell us things that no character could possibly know.
• may make comments about story events and characters.

As you read Irving's story, use this chart to list details that show that the point of view is omniscient.

Different Characters' Thoughts & Experiences	Things No Character Could Know	Comments About Events & Characters

READING STRATEGY
Inferring Cultural Attitudes

Cultural attitudes are the opinions and values of a particular group of people at a particular time. "The Devil and Tom Walker" takes place in colonial America in the 1720s. From the story's details you can **make inferences**, or draw conclusions, about American cultural attitudes at that time. Use a chart like this one to make inferences.

Detail	Cultural Attitude
Oh, I go by various names. . . . I am the wild huntsman in some countries; the black miner in others. In this neighborhood I am known by the name of the black woodsman.	People believed in the Devil and called him by several nicknames.

With each selection, you will study a literary element. It is introduced on the Prepare to Read page. Later, notes in the margins of the selection help you identify this element.

You are also given a reading strategy to use as you read the selection. Notes in the margins of the selection guide you in applying this strategy as you read.

◆ Stop to Reflect

What do you think will happen to Crowninshield? Why?

_____
_____
_____
_____

◆ Reading Strategy

Circle two nicknames for the Devil that are used by people in Walker's area. From the nick-names, what do you **infer** that European colonists associated with the word *black*? Circle the letter of your answer below.

(a) good   (c) poverty

(b) evil   (d) boldness

◆ Literary Analysis

An **omniscient**, or all-knowing, **narrator** tells us the thoughts and attitudes of different characters. Circle Tom's wife's thoughts or attitudes about the treasure. Write one word to describe the wife.

_____

"He's just ready for burning!" said the black man, with a growl of triumph. "You see I am likely to have a good stock of firewood for winter."

"But what right have you," said Tom, "to cut down Deacon Peabody's timber?"

"The right of a <u>prior</u> claim," said the other. "This woodland belonged to me long before one of your white-faced race put foot upon the soil."

"And pray who are you, if I may be so bold?" said Tom.

"Oh, I go by various names, I am the wild huntsman in some countries; the black miner in others. In this neighborhood I am known by the name of the black woodsman. . . ."

"The upshot of all which is, that, if I mistake not," said Tom, sturdily, "you are he commonly called Old Scratch."

"The same, at your service," replied the black man, with a half-civil nod.

◆ ◆ ◆

The Devil offers Tom Captain Kidd's pirate treasure if Tom agrees to his terms. Tom makes no decision. Instead he asks for proof that the Devil is who he says he is. So the Devil presses his finger to Tom's fore-head and then goes off. When Tom gets home, he finds a black thumbprint burned into his forehead. He also learns of the sudden death of Absalom Crowninshield. Convinced he has met the Devil, he tells his wife all about it.

◆ ◆ ◆

All her <u>avarice</u> was awakened at the thought of hidden gold, and she urged her husband to <u>comply</u> with the black man's terms and secure

Vocabulary Development

prior (PRĪ uh) *adj.* previous; from before

avarice (A vuh riz) *adj.* greed

comply (kum PLĪ) *v.* go along with; agree to

REVIEW AND ASSESS

1. Circle the words that best describe Tom Walker.

   greedy   loyal   loving   selfish   lazy

2. What happens to Tom's wife?

   _____
   _____

3. Complete these sentences to explain the bargain that Tom makes.

   Tom agrees to _____

   in exchange for _____.

4. What happens to Tom in the end?

   _____
   _____

5. **Literary Analysis** Show that the story uses **third-person omniscient point of view** by finding examples for the chart below.

Different Characters' Thoughts & Experiences:	Comments About Events & Characters:

from The Iroquois Constitution

Translated by Arthur C. Parker

Summary

This selection is an excerpt, or a section, from *The Iroquois Constitution*. Dekanawidah, who is an Iroquois prophet, speaks here of the Tree of Great Peace that gives shelter and protection to the Iroquois nations. He explains why and how the Five Nations, a group of five Iroquois tribes, should come together to form a union or confederacy for their common good.

Visual Summary

Topic
Putting together a union, or confederate council, of Iroquois nations

Details					
1. ➡	**2.** ➡	**3.** ➡	**4.** ➡	**5.** ➡	**6.**
Tree of Great Peace = Tree of Great Leaves	Tree's roots spread in all directions	Eagle will warn of danger	Council meetings will begin with thanks	String of shells = a pledge to accept the constitution	Hearts of all members filled with peace and goodwill

Main Idea Sentence
Members of the confederate council will be committed to peace for all people, for the present and for future generations.

LITERARY ANALYSIS
Origin Myths

Origin myths are stories about beginnings. These stories are passed down from generation to generation. Many such stories were told and retold long before they were written down.

Origin myths may explain one or more of the following:
- customs, traditions, or social organizations
- natural landmarks such as high mountains
- events beyond people's control, such as earthquakes

This passage from the Iroquois Constitution tells about the founding of a social organization: the alliance between five different Native American nations or peoples.

READING STRATEGY
Recognizing Cultural Details

The ideas, customs, and skills of a particular people or group make up its culture. Literature often reflects the culture that produces it. As you read, **recognizing cultural details** can deepen your understanding. Notice references to objects, animals, or practices that tell you how the people of a culture live or think.

Use the chart below to record two details from the selection. Then tell what each detail tells you about the ideas, customs, or beliefs of the Iroquois.

Detail from the Iroquois Constitution	What It Reveals About Ideas, Customs, or Beliefs
EXAMPLE: planting and naming of the Tree of the Great Peace	• Iroquois put a high value on nature • names have great meaning
1.	
2.	

from The Iroquois Constitution

Translated by Arthur C. Parker

◆ Reading Strategy

Look for the **cultural details** in the bracketed sentence. What do you think the speaker's attitude is toward the cousin lords?

_____

_____

_____

◆ Literary Analysis

Circle two words that show the nature of the Great White Roots in this **origin myth.** What can you tell from this passage about the purpose of the alliance?

_____

_____

◆ Reading Strategy

What role does the eagle play as a **cultural detail** for the Five Nations?

_____

_____

I am Dekanawidah and with the Five Nations[1] underline confederate lords I plant the Tree of the Great Peace. I name the tree the Tree of the Great Long Leaves. Under the shade of this Tree of the Great Peace we spread the soft white feathery down of the globe thistle as seats for you, Adodarhoh, and your cousin lords.

We place you upon those seats, spread soft with the feathery down of the globe thistle, there beneath the shade of the spreading branches of the Tree of Peace. There shall you sit and watch the council fire of the confederacy of the Five Nations, and all the affairs of the Five Nations shall be transacted[2] at this place before you.

Roots have spread out from the Tree of the Great Peace, one to the north, one to the east, one to the south and one to the west. The name of these roots is the Great White Roots and their nature is peace and strength.

◆ ◆ ◆

Other nations wishing to speak with the Five Nations will trace the roots to the tree. Peaceful and obedient people will be welcomed.

◆ ◆ ◆

We place at the top of the Tree of the Long Leaves an eagle who is able to see afar. If he sees in the distance any evil approaching or danger threatening he will at once warn the people of the confederacy.

Vocabulary Development

confederate (kon FED er it) *adj.* united with others for a common purpose

---

1. **Five Nations** the Mohawk, Oneida, Onondaga, Cayuga, and Seneca tribes. Together, these tribes formed the Iroquois Confederation.
2. **transacted** (trans ACT id) *v.* done.

The smoke of the confederate council fire shall ever ascend and pierce the sky so that other nations who may be allies may see the council fire of the Great Peace . . .

◆ **Reading Strategy**

Circle the **cultural details** in the underlined passage that show why the smoke of the council fire will ascend to the sky.

◆ ◆ ◆

The Onondaga lords will open every council meeting by giving thanks to their cousin lords. They will also offer thanks to the earth, the waters, the crops, the trees, the animals, the sun, the moon, and the Great Creator.

◆ ◆ ◆

All lords of the Five Nations' Confederacy must be honest in all things . . . It shall be a serious wrong for anyone to lead a lord into trivial[3] affairs, for the people must ever hold their lords high in estimation[4] out of respect to their honorable positions.

◆ **Stop to Reflect**

What is one requirement for all the lords of the Five Nations?

_____

_____

_____

◆ ◆ ◆

When a new lord joins the council, he must offer a pledge of four strings of shells. The speaker of the council will then welcome the new lord. The lords on the other side of the council fire will receive the pledge. Then they will speak these words to the new lord:

◆ ◆ ◆

"With endless patience you shall carry out your duty and your firmness shall be tempered[5] with tenderness for your people. Neither anger nor fury shall find lodgement in your mind and all your words and actions shall be marked with calm deliberation. In all

◆ **Read Fluently**

Read the bracketed passage aloud. Circle three words that name qualities a new lord should have.

Vocabulary Development

ascend (uh SEND) *v.* rise

deliberation (di lib er A shun) *n.* careful consideration

---

3. **trivial** (TRIV i al) *adj.* unimportant.
4. **estimation** (es ti MA shun) *n.* opinion, judgment.
5. **tempered** (TEM perd) *v.* made more moderate.

of your deliberations in the confederate council, in your efforts at law making, in all your official acts, self-interest shall be cast into oblivion.[6] Cast not over your shoulder behind you the warnings of the nephews and nieces should they chide[7] you for any error or wrong you may do, but return to the way of the Great Law which is just and right. Look and listen for the welfare of the whole people and have always in view not only the present but also the coming generations, even those whose faces are yet beneath the surface of the ground—the unborn of the future nation."

6. **oblivion** (uh BLIV i un) *n.* forgetfulness.
7. **chide** (CHĪD) *v.* criticize.

◆ **Reading Strategy**

What attitude about the future do the members of the speaker's **culture** have?

_____

_____

_____

1. What three actions does the speaker perform in the first paragraph? List them on the chart.

   First Paragraph

   Action 1: _____

   Action 2: _____

   Action 3: _____

2. Why is it important for an eagle to be placed at the top of the Great Tree?

   _____

   _____

3. According to the speaker, what attitude should the people have about their lords?

   _____

   _____

4. **Literary Analysis:** An **origin myth** is a story about beginnings. What beginning does this decree help to explain?

   _____

   _____

5. **Reading Strategy:** When you **recognize cultural details**, you relate a literary selection to the culture that produced it. What do the qualities and conduct required of council lords tell you about Iroquois society and its values?

   _____

   _____

Listening and Speaking

A Dramatic Reading

The Iroquois Constitution describes how a new Iroquois lord should join the council. With two other students, plan a dramatic reading of this process.

1. Assign the roles
   - Who will play the role of Dekanawidah? This student will read all the main sections that have no quotation marks.

   _____

   - Who will play the role of a narrator? This student will read the sections that are indented and set off with diamonds.

   _____

   - Who will play the role of the speaker of the council? This student will read the last paragraph, which is in quotation marks.

   _____

2. Plan the reading.
   - What will you use as props, or items that you will hold during your dramatic reading?

   _____

   - Where will you sit, walk, or stand as you perform?

   _____

3. Rehearse your reading several times to learn your roles.
   - What changes do you need to make in your plan after your first rehearsal?

   _____

4. Present your reading to your class.
5. Answer your classmates' questions about the Iroquois Constitution or about your reading.

from The Interesting Narrative of the Life of Olaudah Equiano

Olaudah Equiano

Summary

This excerpt, or section, from a slave narrative tells of the experiences of a young slave during the middle passage, or the trip across the ocean. Olaudah Equiano describes the horrors of the journey, telling of the sickening smells in the hold of the ship, where people are so crowded they can hardly turn around. He tells about the cruelty of the whites, who starve the captives and keep them in chains. When two captives jump overboard, preferring death to slavery, one is saved and then whipped badly for trying to escape. Equiano also tells of seeing flying fishes during the journey and of being shown how to use a quadrant, an instrument that determines the position of a ship. When they arrive in Bridgetown, the captives are put into small groups to be examined by people who plan to buy them.

Visual Summary

Main Idea

Conditions on slave ships from Africa cause many slaves to die during the journey.

The smell of the ship is terrible.	The ship's crew is cruel.	Many slaves die.
perspiration	slaves are chained	some become sick from the filth and smells
no fresh air	slaves beaten for trying to escape	some jump into the sea

LITERARY ANALYSIS
Slave Narratives

In an autobiography, a writer tells the true story of his or her own life. A **slave narrative** is an autobiographical account of the life of a slave. Slave narratives are often written to show the horrors of slavery.

For example, Olaudah Equiano gives this description of the harsh conditions on the ship that brought him to Barbados:

> The shrieks of the women, and the groans of the dying, rendered the whole a scene of horror almost inconceivable.

As you read, look for other details that describe the horrors of the voyage.

READING STRATEGY
Summarizing

When your reading is challenging, it is often useful to **summarize** the main points. When you summarize, you use your own words to state briefly the main ideas and details of the text. A good summary is always much shorter than the original passage.

To summarize, make a diagram like the one shown, which summarizes Equiano's first paragraph. As you read, write notes like these to help you summarize Equiano's ideas.

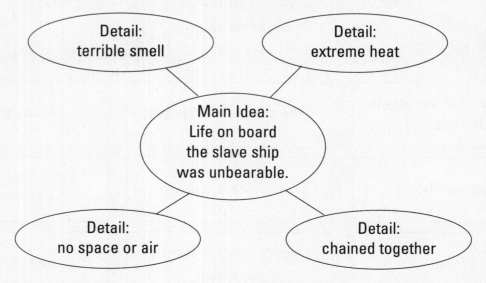

Summary: The heat, the foul air, the cramped quarters, and the chains all combined to make life on board the slave ship unbearable.

from The Interesting Narrative of the Life of Olaudah Equiano

Olaudah Equiano

At last when the ship we were in, had got in all her cargo, they made ready with many fearful noises, and we were all put under deck, so that we could not see how they managed the vessel. But this disappointment was the least of my sorrow. The stench of the hold while we were on the coast was so intolerably <u>loathsome</u>, that it was dangerous to remain there for any time, and some of us had been permitted to stay on the deck for the fresh air; but now that the whole ship's cargo were confined together, it became absolutely <u>pestilential</u>. The closeness of the place, and the heat of the climate, added to the number in the ship, which was so crowded that each had scarcely room to turn himself, almost suffocated us. This produced <u>copious</u> perspirations, so that the air soon became unfit for respiration, from a variety of loathsome smells, and brought on a sickness among the slaves, of which many died—thus falling victims to the <u>improvident</u> <u>avarice</u>, as I may call it, of their purchasers. This wretched situation was again aggravated by the galling[1] of the chains, now become insupportable, and the filth of the necessary tubs, into which the children often fell, and were almost suffocated. The shrieks of the women, and the groans of the dying,

◆ **Literary Analysis**

Underline three details in this **slave narrative** that show the horrible conditions for the slaves on board ship.

◆ **Stop to Reflect**

Why would it have been in the interest of the slave traders to treat the slaves better?

_____

_____

_____

Vocabulary Development

loathsome (LOHTH suhm) *adj.* hateful
pestilential (pes ti LEN shuhl) *adj.* likely to cause disease
copious (KO pee uhs) *adj.* plentiful
improvident (im PRAH vuh duhnt) *adj.* shortsighted
avarice (AV uh ris) *n.* greed for riches

---

1. **galling** (GAWL ing) *n.* the creation of sores by rubbing or chafing.

rendered the whole a scene of horror almost inconceivable.

◆ ◆ ◆

Equiano envied the fish of the sea for their freedom. During the voyage, he grew more fearful of the white slavers' cruelty.

◆ ◆ ◆

One day they had taken a number of fishes; and when they had killed and satisfied themselves with as many as they thought fit, to our astonishment who were on deck, rather than give any of them to us to eat, as we expected, they tossed the remaining fish into the sea again, although we begged and prayed for some as well as we could, but in vain.

◆ ◆ ◆

Some of the hungry slaves tried to get fish in secret. They were discovered and whipped. Then three desperate slaves jumped into the sea. The others were immediately put below deck. Two of the slaves drowned. The third was rescued and then beaten unmercifully.

◆ ◆ ◆

During our passage, I first saw flying fishes, which surprised me very much; they used frequently to fly across the ship, and many of them fell on the deck. I also now first saw the use of the quadrant;[2] I had often with astonishment seen the mariners make observations with it, and I could not think what it meant. They at last took notice of my surprise; and one of them, willing to increase it, as well as to gratify my curiosity, made me one day look through it. The clouds appeared to me to be land, which disappeared as they passed along. This heightened my wonder; and I was now more persuaded than ever, that I

---

2. **quadrant** (KWAH druhnt) *n.* an instrument used by navigators to determine a ship's position.

◆ **Reading Strategy**

Summarize the first bracketed section in your own words.

_____

_____

_____

_____

_____

◆ **Reading Check**

Underline the parts of the summary that show what some slaves do to escape the misery of the journey.

◆ **Read Fluently**

Read the second bracketed passage aloud. Circle the two sights that attract Equiano's curiosity.

was in another world, and that every thing about me was magic.

◆　◆　◆

The ship anchored off Bridgetown, the capital of the island of Barbados in the West Indies. Merchants and planters came on board to examine the slaves. The slaves on the ship were fearful, but some older slaves came from the land to reassure them. Finally, the slaves went ashore.

◆　◆　◆

We were <u>conducted</u> immediately to the merchant's yard, where we were all pent up together, like so many sheep in a fold, without regard to sex or age. . . . We were not many days in the merchant's <u>custody,</u> before we were sold after their usual manner, which is this: On a signal given (as the beat of a drum), the buyers rush at once into the yard where the slaves are confined, and make choice of that parcel[3] they like best. . . .

◆ **Stop to Reflect**

In the last paragraph of this **slave narrative**, what is the effect of these details on the reader's emotions?

_____

_____

_____

_____

_____

_____

Vocabulary Development

conducted (kuhn DUHK tuhd) *v.* led
custody (KUHS tuh dee) *n.* keeping, possession

3. **parcel** (PAR suhl) *n.* group.

1. Why does Equiano blame the deaths of many slaves on the "improvident avarice" of the traders?

_____

2. What happens when the traders catch a number of fish?

_____

_____

3. What happens when the traders recover the slave who had jumped overboard?

_____

_____

4. **Reading Strategy:** When you **summarize** a passage, you use your own words to state briefly the main idea and the key details. Summarize the passage about the flying fish and the quadrant.

_____

_____

5. What do you think the details about the flying fish and the quadrant show about the young Equiano's personality?

_____

_____

6. **Literary Analysis:** The purpose of a **slave narrative** is often to show the horrors of bondage. What details in the description of life in the merchant's yard in Bridgetown contribute to this purpose?

_____

_____

Writing

A Museum Placard

Museum exhibits usually include **placards**, or signs that identify the items on display. Sometimes a large placard is placed at the beginning of an exhibit. The purpose of this placard is to introduce visitors to the exhibit and to educate them about it.

Recently, some museums have been presenting exhibits to show the historical facts of the slave trade. Write the introductory information for a placard that visitors will read at the beginning of an exhibit on the slave trade. On your placard, explain the sequence of events that happened to slaves like Olaudah Equiano.

Follow these guidelines to write your placard:
* Use the text of Equiano's narrative to gather facts. Also use library sources, such as encyclopedias and history books.

1. How were the slaves captured?

_____

2. What were the events during the voyage?

_____

3. What events happened after the slave ships landed?

_____

* Plan a graphic display for your placard like the one shown below. This graphic display organizes key events in time order.

Model: Organizing Events in Time Order		
How were the slaves captured?	What were the events during the voyage?	What events happened after the slave ships landed?

* Check that your placard gives information about the stages of the slave trade. Revise any confusing shifts in time order.
* Use a large piece of construction paper to create your placard. Display it on the bulletin board in your classroom.

from The General History of Virginia

John Smith

Summary

This excerpt tells of the hardships of the Jamestown colony. Fifty colonists die between May and September. When Captain John Smith goes on an expedition, he and his men are attacked by Indians. Smith's life is spared because he gives the Indians his compass and because Pocahontas, Chief Powhatan's daughter, saves him. After six weeks as a captive, Smith is allowed to return to Jamestown. Pocahontas brings the settlers food, saving their lives.

Visual Summary

Topic
The first months of the Jamestown settlement

Sequence					
1. →	2. →	3. →	4. →	5. →	6.
After the ship leaves, the settlers do not have enough food.	The settlers work so hard that they become weak.	Fifty people die between May and September.	John Smith is taken prisoner by Indians.	Pocahontas saves John Smith's life.	Pocahontas brings the settlers food and saves their lives.

Main Idea Sentence
Despite the great challenges to the Jamestown settlement and to John Smith, the settlement survives.

LITERARY ANALYSIS
Narrative Accounts

A **narrative account** tells the story of real-life events. Some historical narratives, including *The General History of Virginia*, are firsthand accounts, also called primary sources. John Smith actually lived through the events that he describes. For example, Smith tells here about his responsibilities in the new colony:

> The new President and Martin, being little beloved, of weak judgment in dangers, and less industry in peace, committed the managing of all things abroad to Captain Smith . . .

Other historical narratives are written by people who did not experience the events. The writers of these accounts depend on research, rather than on firsthand observation. These narratives are called secondary sources.

Firsthand accounts, or primary sources, are valuable for historians because the writers are close to the story. On the other hand, because of the writer's personal involvement, firsthand accounts are not always objective. As you read, look for factual information that Smith saw or heard firsthand. Also think about whether the information is objective.

READING STRATEGY
Breaking Down Sentences

You can increase your understanding of a text by **breaking down sentences**. Consider one part of a sentence at a time. Look at a long sentence, and separate its most important parts from the difficult language until you get to the main idea.

The most important parts of any sentence are the *who* and the *did what*. The *who* is the subject. The *did what* is the main verb.

As you read, use the diagram below to help you figure out the meaning of long, complicated sentences.

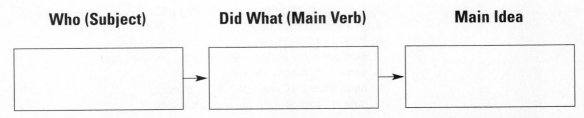

Who (Subject) → **Did What (Main Verb)** → **Main Idea**

from The General History of Virginia
John Smith

What Happened Till the First Supply

Being thus left to our fortunes, it fortuned[1] that within ten days, scarce ten amongst us could either go[2] or well stand, such extreme weakness and sickness oppressed us. And thereat none need marvel if they consider the cause and reason, which was this: While the ships stayed, our allowance was somewhat bettered by a daily proportion of biscuit which the sailors would <u>pilfer</u> to sell, give, or exchange with us for money, sassafras,[3] or furs. But when they departed, there remained neither tavern, beer house, nor place of relief but the common kettle.[4] Had we been as free from all sins as <u>gluttony</u> and drunkenness we might have been canonized[5] for saints, but our President[6] would never have been admitted for engrossing to his private,[7] oatmeal, sack,[8] oil, aqua vitae,[9] beef, eggs, or what not but the kettle; that indeed he allowed equally to be distributed, and that was half a pint of wheat and as much barley boiled with water for a man a day, and this, having fried some twenty-six weeks in the ship's hold,[10] contained as many worms as grains so that we

◆ **Read Fluently**

Read the bracketed passage aloud. How do things change after the ships leave?

_____

_____

_____

Vocabulary Development

pilfer (PIL fer) *v.* steal

gluttony (GLUT un nee) *n.* habit of eating too much

---

1. **fortuned** *v.* happened.
2. **go** *v.* be active.
3. **sassafras** (SAS uh fras) *n.* a tree, the root of which was valued for its use as medicine.
4. **common kettle** communal cooking pot.
5. **canonized** (KAN uh nizd) *v.* made a saint.
6. **President Wingfield,** the leader of the colony.
7. **engrossing to his private** taking for his own use.
8. **sack** *n.* type of white wine.
9. **aqua vitae** (AK wuh VI tee) *n.* brandy.
10. **hold** *n.* storage area for a ship's cargo.

might truly call it rather so much bran than corn; our drink was water, our lodgings castles in the air.

◆ ◆ ◆

That summer fifty colonists die, and another President is elected. Suddenly the fortunes of the settlers change. The Indians bring them food. Smith blames the hard times on the colonists' ignorance. They thought the sea journey would take two months and it took five. So supplies run short.

◆ ◆ ◆

Such actions have ever since the world's beginning been subject to such accidents, and everything of worth is found full of difficulties, but nothing so difficult as to establish a commonwealth so far remote from men and means and where men's minds are so untoward[11] as neither do well themselves nor suffer others. But to proceed.

The new President and Martin, being little beloved, of weak judgment in dangers, and less industry in peace, committed the managing of all things abroad[12] to Captain Smith, who, by his own example, good words, and fair promises, set some to mow, others to bind thatch, some to build houses, others to thatch them, himself always bearing the greatest task for his own share, so that in short time he provided most of them lodgings, neglecting any for himself. . . .

◆ ◆ ◆

Leading an expedition on the Chickahominy River, Smith and his men are attacked by Indians. Smith is held prisoner for six or seven weeks. Several times he is on the point of being killed. However, he gains the favor of the Indian leader, who finally brings him to Powhatan.

◆ ◆ ◆

---

11. **untoward** *adj.* stubborn.
12. **abroad** *adv.* outside the perimeter fence.

◆ **Reading Check**

Why is the corn spoiled?

_____

_____

_____

◆ **Reading Strategy**

Break down the underlined **long sentence**. Circle the part of the sentence that states the main idea.

Mark the Text

◆ **Literary Analysis**

Circle two phrases in this part of Smith's **narrative account** that might be examples of reporting that is not objective.

Mark the Text

Break down the bracketed **sentence**. List five factual details that Smith gives to describe this scene.

_____

_____

_____

_____

_____

At last they brought him to Werowocomoco, where was Powhatan, their Emperor. Here more than two hundred of those grim courtiers stood wondering at him, as he had been a monster, till Powhatan and his train had put themselves in their greatest braveries.[13] Before a fire upon a seat like a bedstead, he sat covered with a great robe made of raccoon skins and all the tails hanging by. On either hand did sit a young wench[14] of sixteen or eighteen years and along on each side the house, two rows of men and behind them as many women, with all their heads and shoulders painted red, many of their heads bedecked[15] with the white down of birds, and a great chain of white beads about their necks.

At his entrance before the King, all the people gave a great shout. The queen of Appomattoc was appointed to bring him water to wash his hands, and another brought him a bunch of feathers, instead of a towel, to dry them; having feasted him after their best barbarous manner they could, a long consultation was held, but the conclusion was, two great stones were brought before Powhatan: then as many as could, laid hands on him, dragged him to them, and thereon laid his head and being ready with their clubs to beat out his brains, Pocahontas, the King's dearest daughter, when no <u>entreaty</u> could prevail, got his head in her arms and laid her own upon his to save him from death; whereat the Emperor was contented he should live to make him hatchets, and her bells, beads, and copper, for they thought him as well of all occupations as themselves.[16]

◆ ◆ ◆

Vocabulary Development

entreaty (en TREE tee) *n.* plea or prayer

---

13. **braveries** (BRAY vuh reez) *n.* fine dress.
14. **wench** *n.* young woman.
15. **bedecked** (bee DEKT) *v.* decorated.
16. **as well . . . themselves** capable of making them just as well as they could themselves.

Powhatan and Smith become friends. The Indian emperor offers to sell the colonists land in exchange for guns and a grindstone. Smith returns to Jamestown and sends cannons and a millstone back to Powhatan. When some of the colonists try to turn back to England, Smith prevents them by force. He is also able to defeat a plot against him by the President and some other settlers.

◆   ◆   ◆

Now every once in four or five days, Pocahontas with her attendants brought him so much provision that saved many of their lives, that else for all this had starved with hunger.

His relation of the plenty he had seen, especially at Werowocomoco, and of the state and bounty of Powhatan (which till that time was unknown), so revived their dead spirits (especially the love of Pocahontas) as all men's fear was abandoned.

Thus you may see what difficulties still crossed any good endeavor; and the good success of the business being thus oft brought to the very period of destruction; yet you see by what strange means God hath still delivered it.

◆ Reading Check

Underline two parts of the bracketed passage that explain why the colonists were no longer afraid.

◆ Read Fluently

Read the last paragraph aloud. Who or what does Smith say is responsible for the "good success of the business"?

_____

_____

_____

1. According to Smith, why were the colonists so weak and sickly?

_____

_____

2. When Powhatan was about to execute Smith, who saved him?

_____

_____

3. What agreement did Powhatan reach with Smith?

_____

_____

4. **Literary Analysis:** In a firsthand **narrative account**, the writer is personally involved in events. Give one example of the way Smith praises his own good qualities.

_____

_____

5. **Reading Strategy:** You can often find the main idea by **breaking down** a long, difficult sentence. Look back at the selection and choose two sentences that you found challenging. Write them in the chart. Locate the *who* and the *did what* in each sentence. Then, write the meaning of the sentences as you understand them.

Sentence 1	Sentence 2

Who (Subject)	Did What (Main Verb)	Who (Subject)	Did What (Main Verb)

Main Idea	Main Idea

Listening and Speaking

Persuasive Speech

In a **persuasive speech**, you try to convince your listeners to think or behave a certain way. Good persuasion uses many different tools. For example, a speaker may support a position with **logical appeals**:

Logical Appeals

/ | \

Facts   Examples   Reasons

Persuasive speakers also use **emotional appeals**. A speaker may appeal to the feelings of the audience, such as pride or fear. Certain words, like *love, victory, country,* or *glory,* are charged with strong emotional associations.

Put yourself in the position of Captain John Smith. As Smith, deliver a persuasive speech to the colonists in favor of remaining in Virginia and making an alliance with Powhatan. As you plan your speech, answer these questions:

- What are the hardships that the colonists have overcome so far?

_____

- In what ways has Powhatan already shown friendship?

_____

- What provisions and land does the Indian leader have under his control?

_____

- How is staying in Virginia in the best interest of the settlers themselves?

_____

- What are the likely needs of the colonists in the future?

_____

Now organize and write your speech in a way that makes sense, using both logical and emotional appeals. Then present your speech to the class and ask for their feedback.

from Sinners in the Hands of an Angry God

Jonathan Edwards

Summary

This excerpt from Edwards's sermon describes God's rising anger against the sinners in the congregation. These sinners, Edwards says, are like spiders that their angry God holds over hell. Edwards tells his listeners that they can save their souls from everlasting suffering only if they beg God for forgiveness now and experience the saving grace of conversion, which will give them a place among the elect, or those chosen by God.

Visual Summary

Purpose	Details to Achieve This Purpose
To motivate listeners to convert and save their souls	• Only the power of God holds you up. • Black clouds of God's anger hang over your heads. • Only God's pleasure keeps you from being destroyed forever. • Sinners are in great danger. • You have nothing that can persuade God to spare you. • God will not pity you. • Today the door of mercy is open.

LITERARY ANALYSIS

Sermon

A **sermon** is usually a speech given by a preacher in a house of worship. Sermons are normally part of a religious service.

A sermon is an example of persuasion. Persuasion tries to convince listeners or readers to adopt a particular opinion or to act in a certain way. As you read, keep in mind these features of an effective sermon:

- It touches the emotions of listeners.
- It inspires listeners to take action.
- It addresses the needs and concerns of the audience.
- It uses colorful and rhythmic language.

READING STRATEGY

Using Context Clues

You can often understand the meaning of unfamiliar words by **using context clues**. A word's context is its surrounding words, phrases, and sentences. For example, suppose you want to find the meaning of the word *abominable* in this passage from Jonathan Edwards's sermon:

> You are ten thousand times more *abominable* in his [God's] eyes than the most hateful venomous serpent is in ours. . . .

The context clue here is in the form of a comparison. Edwards says that the way a sinner looks in God's eyes is like the way a hateful snake looks in our eyes. From this clue, you can guess that *abominable* must be close in meaning to horrible or *disgusting*.

Use this chart to define other difficult words by using context clues.

Word	Context Clues	Meaning

from Sinners in the Hands of an Angry God

Jonathan Edwards

from Sinners in the Hands
of an Angry God
Jonathan Edwards

◆ Literary Analysis

Underline two words in the **sermon's** title that suggest the emotional focus of Edwards's message.

◆ Reading Strategy

Circle the **context clues** that help you understand the meaning of *gaping*. What does *gaping* mean?

_____

_____

_____

◆ Stop to Reflect

To what does Edwards compare the wrath of God?

_____

_____

_____

The author, Jonathan Edwards, directs his sermon toward those with whom God is not pleased. He talks about a world of misery for them.

◆ ◆ ◆

There is the dreadful pit of the glowing flames of the <u>wrath</u> of God; there is Hell's wide <u>gaping</u> mouth open; and you have nothing to stand upon, nor anything to take hold of; there is nothing between you and Hell but the air; it is only the power and mere pleasure of God that holds you up.

◆ ◆ ◆

Sinners may think they are kept out of Hell by their own life and strength, but they are wrong. Sinners are like heavy weights of lead. If God chose to let them go, they would sink straight to Hell. God's anger is like a terrible storm, held back for the moment.
God's wrath is like a stream that is dammed. The longer it is dammed, the stronger the waters will be once the dam is opened.

◆ ◆ ◆

It is true, that judgment against your evil works has not been executed hitherto;[1] the Hoods of God's vengeance have been withheld; but your guilt in the meantime is constantly increasing, and you are every day treasuring up more wrath; the waters are constantly rising, and <u>waxing</u> more and more mighty; and

---

Vocabulary Development

wrath (RATH) *n.* great anger
waxing (WAKS ing) *v.* increasing

---

1. **hitherto** (hi thuhr TOO) *adv.* up to now.

there is nothing but the mere pleasure of God, that holds the waters back, that are unwilling to be stopped, and press hard to go forward.

◆　◆　◆

God's hand is holding the gate that controls the dam. If he should decide to move his hand, the flood of anger would be unbelievable. No human strength, or even the strength of the devil, could stop it.

◆　◆　◆

The bow of God's wrath is bent, and the arrow made ready on the string, and justice bends the arrow at your heart, and strains the bow, and it is nothing but the mere pleasure of God, and that of an angry God, without any promise or obligation at all, that keeps the arrow one moment from being made drunk with your blood.

◆　◆　◆

Everyone who does not repent risks being destroyed. Sinners may not believe that they are in danger now. There will come a time, though, when they will be convinced.

◆　◆　◆

The God that holds you over the pit of Hell, much as one holds a spider, or some loath-some insect over the fire, abhors you, and is dreadfully provoked: his wrath towards you burns like fire; he looks upon you as worthy of nothing else, but to be cast into the fire; he is

◆ **Reading Check**

What is holding the waters back?

_____

_____

_____

◆ **Read Fluently**

Read the bracketed paragraph aloud. Then fill in the blanks below.

1. The wrath of God is like a

_____

that is bent.

2. Justice directs the

_____

to the heart of the sinner.

　　from Sinners in the Hands of an Angry God　**29**

_____

_____

_____

◆ Stop to Reflect

Circle the word that Edwards keeps repeating in the bracketed passage. Why do you think he emphasizes this word?

_____

_____

of purer eyes than to bear to have you in his sight; you are ten thousand times more <u>abominable</u> in his eyes, than the most hateful <u>venomous</u> serpent is in ours. . . .

◆ ◆ ◆

Edwards warns sinners that they are in great danger. God is as angry with them as he is with those already in Hell.

◆ ◆ ◆

You hang by a slender thread, with the flames of divine wrath flashing about it, and ready every moment to singe it, and burn it <u>asunder</u>; and you have no interest in any mediator, and nothing to lay hold of to save yourself, nothing to keep off the flames of wrath, nothing of your own, nothing that you ever have done, nothing that you can do, to <u>induce</u> God to spare you one moment. . . .

◆ ◆ ◆

Edwards says that God will have no mercy on sinners who do not repent. However, the punishments of sinners will be just. If sinners repent now, God will show them mercy. If they refuse to repent, they will be tormented forever. Sinners who do not repent are in daily and hourly danger. Think of those who are now suffering endless misery in Hell. They have no more chances to obtain salvation. But those who are still alive may still be saved.

Vocabulary Development

abominable (uh BAHM uh nuh buhl) *adj.* hateful, disgusting
venomous (VEN uh muhs) *adj.* poisonous
asunder (a SUN duhr) *adv.* apart
induce (in DOOS) *v.* persuade

Sinners now have a wonderful opportunity to gain forgiveness. They can save their souls from everlasting suffering. Many other sinners are <u>flocking</u> to him and entering his kingdom. They are coming from everywhere. These sinners had been miserable, but now God has washed their sins away and they are rejoicing. It would be awful to be left behind and not join in this joyful celebration. Edwards says all sinners in his <u>congregation</u> should escape God's wrath and experience the saving grace of conversion.

◆　◆　◆

"Haste and escape for your lives, look not behind you, escape to the mountain, lest you be consumed."[2]

◆ **Reading Strategy**

Circle the **context clues** that help you determine the meaning of *flocking*. What does *flocking* mean?

_____

_____

_____

◆ **Literary Analysis**

According to the bracketed summary of this persuasive **sermon**, what does Edwards want the congregation to do?

_____

_____

_____

◆ **Reading Check**

Underline the quotation from the Bible. Why is the Biblical quotation appropriate for Edwards's sermon?

_____

_____

_____

Vocabulary Development

congregation (kahn gruh GAY shuhn) *n.* members of a place of worship

---

2. **"Haste . . . consumed"** from Genesis 19:17, the angels' warning to Lot, the only virtuous man in Sodom, to flee the city before they destroy it.

1. According to the first paragraph, what keeps sinners from falling into Hell?

_____

_____

2. On the chart below, identify two images from nature that Edwards uses to describe the anger of God.

	Image 1	Image 2
God's anger is like:	_____	_____

3. Toward the end of the sermon, what does Edwards say that sinners can obtain, and how can they obtain it?

_____

_____

4. **Literary Analysis:** In a **sermon**, the speaker wants to persuade listeners to adopt a definite point of view. What emotions in his listeners does Edwards hope to touch in this sermon?

_____

_____

5. **Reading Strategy:** You can often guess the meaning of difficult words by **using context clues**, or clues from nearby words, phrases, and sentences. Use context clues to define the italicized words:

(a) "The God that holds you over the pit of Hell, much as one holds a spider, or some loathsome insect over the fire, *abhors* you, and is dreadfully provoked. . . ."

Definition of *abhor*: _____

(b) "To see so many others feasting, while you are *pining* and perishing!"

Definition of *pining*: _____

Writing

Evaluation of Persuasion

When you **evaluate** something, you use standards to judge its worth or effectiveness. In his sermon, Jonathan Edwards uses persuasion to convey a definite point of view. Write an **evaluation of persuasion** to judge how effective the sermon is. As you plan your evaluation, consider the following questions.

- What is Edwards's *purpose* in the sermon?

_____

- Who is the *audience* for the sermon, and what is the occasion?

_____

- What powerful *images* does Edwards use?

_____

- What *emotions* in the audience does the sermon appeal to?

_____

1. Begin your evaluation with a general statement about the sermon's effectiveness.

_____

_____

2. Identify specific examples.
   - Quote lines from the text that show Edwards appealing to fear and guilt.

_____

   - Identify the specific images from nature that Edwards uses.

_____

3. At the end of your evaluation, summarize or restate your main idea.

_____

_____

4. Now read over your essay as if you were seeing it for the first time. Cut out any information that is not related to the main idea.
5. Share your essay with your classmates. Find out if they agree with your evaluation.

from Sinners in the Hands of an Angry God **33**

from The Autobiography
Benjamin Franklin

Summary

In this excerpt from his autobiography, Franklin describes his plan for achieving moral perfection by listing thirteen virtues. He plans to work on one virtue at a time, recording his progress in a notebook. He makes seven columns on a page, one for each day of the week. He makes thirteen rows on the page, one for each virtue. Each day, he marks with a black spot every fault he commits. For each week, he works on one virtue and tries to keep that virtue's row free of black marks. He finds his plan helpful but not completely successful.

Visual Summary

Goal: Moral perfection		
Methods		
List of virtues	**Notebook**	**Daily schedule**
• temperance • silence • order • resolution • frugality • industry • sincerity • justice • moderation • cleanliness • tranquillity • chastity • humility	• one page for each virtue • seven columns on each page, one for each day of the week • thirteen rows, one for each virtue • black mark in proper row and column for each fault • one week's attention to one virtue at a time	• 5:00 A.M.–7:00 A.M.: Rise, wash, pray, plan the day, review the virtues, and eat breakfast • 9:00 A.M.: Begin work • NOON: Read, review accounts, and dine • 3:00 P.M.: Continue work • 6:00 P.M.: Put things in their places • 8:00 P.M.: Supper, music or diversion, examine the day • 1:00 A.M.: Sleep
Result: "... though I never arrived at the perfection I had been so ambitious of obtaining, but fell far short of it, yet I was, by the endeavor, a better and happier man ..."		

LITERARY ANALYSIS
Autobiography
What is an **autobiography**?
- An **autobiography** is the story of a person's life.
- It is told by the person.
- The pronoun *I* is used throughout.
- An autobiography can give personal views of history.

In this section of his *Autobiography,* Franklin tells about his system for forming good habits. He finds that it is not as easy as he thought. But he keeps trying. He never becomes perfect, but he finds that he is happy just to try. In the following passage, Franklin explains how difficult the task is.

> But I soon found I had undertaken a task of more difficulty than I had imagined. While my care was employed in guarding against one fault, I was often surprised by another.

READING STRATEGY
Drawing Conclusions
When you read an autobiography, look beyond just what the person is saying. Ask yourself, "What does this tell us about the person?" Then you can **draw conclusions** about what kind of person the writer is. On the chart below, list three statements that Franklin makes about himself. Then explain what each statement tells you about Franklin. When you finish reading, use this information to draw conclusions about Franklin's character.

Statement by Franklin	What It Tells About Him
EX: "I therefore contrived the following method."	He likes to use methods to get things done.

from The Autobiography **35**

◆ **Reading Strategy**

Which phrases in the bracketed paragraph help you **draw conclusions** about Franklin's character? Circle them.

Franklin decides to take up a difficult project. He will try to live a perfect life. He knows, or thinks he knows, what is right and wrong. He doesn't see why he cannot always do the one and avoid the other.

◆ ◆ ◆

But I soon found I had undertaken a task of more difficulty than I had imagined. While my care was employed in guarding against one fault, I was often surprised by another. . . . I therefore contrived the following method.

◆ ◆ ◆

Franklin has read other people's lists of virtues in the past. These lists don't seem quite right to him. He writes his own list of thirteen virtues. He adds short notes. The notes explain what the virtue means to him. Here is his list.

◆ ◆ ◆

◆ **Stop to Reflect**

Franklin makes a list to organize his plan. What does this show about his character?

_____
_____
_____
_____

1. TEMPERANCE Eat not to dullness; drink not to elevation.
2. SILENCE Speak not but what may benefit others or yourself; avoid trifling conversation.
3. ORDER Let all your things have their places; let each part of your business have its time.
4. RESOLUTION Resolve to perform what you ought; perform without fail what you resolve.
5. FRUGALITY Make no expense but to do good to others or yourself; i.e., waste nothing.
6. INDUSTRY Lose no time; be always employed in something useful; cut off all unnecessary actions.
7. SINCERITY Use no hurtful deceit; think innocently and justly, and, if you speak, speak accordingly.

◆ **Reading Check**

What is Franklin's attitude about wasting time? Circle the answer.

8. JUSTICE Wrong none by doing injuries, or omitting the benefits that are your duty.

9. MODERATION Avoid extremes; forebear resenting injuries so much as you think they deserve.

10. CLEANLINESS Tolerate no uncleanliness in body, clothes, or habitation.

11. <u>TRANQUILLITY Be not disturbed at trifles, or at accidents common or unavoidable.</u>

12. CHASTITY

13. HUMILITY Imitate Jesus and Socrates.

♦ ♦ ♦

◆ **Reading Strategy**

What might Franklin say to someone who was very upset about a minor traffic accident? **Draw conclusions** from the underlined text.

_____

_____

_____

Franklin's goal is to get into the habit of all these virtues. He tries one at a time, then goes on to the next. He thinks that some virtues might make other ones easier. That is why he lists *Temperance* first. Temperance helps you keep a clear head. A clear head helps you guard against bad habits. With the habit of temperance, *Silence* would be easier.

◆ **Reading Strategy**

What **conclusions** can you **draw** from the bracketed text about the values of the time? Complete this sentence with your answer.

In Franklin's day, people thought virtues such as _____ and _____ were good to have.

He also wants to gain knowledge. He knows that knowledge is obtained more by listening than by speaking. He gives *Silence* the second place. This virtue and the next, *Order,* would give him more time for his studies. *Resolution* is next. It will help Franklin stick to his plan. *Frugality* and *Industry* will help him pay all his debts. They will also help him add to his wealth. Then it will be easier to practice *Sincerity* and *Justice,* and so on. He decides to check his progress every day.

◆ **Reading Strategy**

How does Franklin think we add to our knowledge? Circle the answer that helps you **draw a conclusion**.

♦ ♦ ♦

I made a little book, in which I <u>allotted</u> a page for each of the virtues. I ruled each page with red ink, so as to have seven columns, one

---

Vocabulary Development

allotted (uh LOT ted) *v.* assigned, gave a part

---

for each day of the week, marking each column with a letter for the day. I crossed these columns with thirteen red lines, marking the beginning of each line with the first letter of one of the virtues, on which line and in its proper column I might mark, by a little black spot, every fault I found upon examination to have been committed respecting that virtue upon that day.

◆ ◆ ◆

He decides to spend a week on each virtue. In the first week, he practices Temperance. His goal the first week is to keep his first line, marked T, clear of spots. The next week, he might try the next virtue. He will try to keep both lines clear of spots. He can go through the whole list in thirteen weeks, and he repeats this process four times a year.

Franklin follows his plan for some time. One thing surprises him. He has more faults than he had imagined. But he is glad to see them become less and less. After a while, he goes through only one course in a year. Later, he goes through one in several years. At last, he stops doing it. He is too busy with trips and business in Europe. But he always carries his little book with him.

The virtue of Order gives him the most trouble. He just isn't used to putting papers and things in their places. He has a very good memory. So he can always remember where he has left something.

◆ ◆ ◆

This article, therefore, cost me so much painful attention, and my faults in it <u>vexed</u> me so much, and I made so little progress in

Vocabulary Development

vexed (VEKST) *v.* annoyed, bothered

amendment, and had such frequent relapses, that I was almost ready to give up the attempt, and content myself with a faulty character in that respect, like the man who, in buying an ax of a smith,[1] my neighbor, desired to have the whole of its surface as bright as the edge. The smith consented to grind it bright for him if he would turn the wheel; he turned, while the smith pressed the broad face of the ax hard and heavily on the stone, which made the turning of it very fatiguing. The man came every now and then from the wheel to see how the work went on, and at length would take his ax as it was, without farther grinding. "No," said the smith, "turn on, turn on; we shall have it bright by and by; as yet, it is only speckled." "Yes," says the man, *"but I think I like a speckled ax best."*

◆ ◆ ◆

Franklin believes that many people are like this man. Some people find it too difficult to form good habits. They just give up the struggle. They decide that "a speckled ax is best." Franklin is the same way about the virtue of Order. He thinks that other people might envy or hate him if he becomes perfect. He thinks that a good man should keep a few faults. This way, he can keep his friends.

◆ ◆ ◆

In truth, I found myself incorrigible with respect to Order; and now I am grown old, and

◆ **Reading Strategy**

Here, Franklin tells a story about a man with an ax. What **conclusion** can you **draw** from this story about Franklin's sense of humor?

_____

_____

_____

◆ **Reading Check**

Why does Franklin think a good man should keep a few faults?

_____

_____

_____

_____

Vocabulary Development

amendment (uh MEND ment) *n.* improvement, correction

relapses (REE lap ses) *n.* slips back to a former state

fatiguing (fuh TEEG ing) *adj.* tiring

speckled (SPEK uhld) *adj.* covered with small spots

incorrigible (in KOR ij uh buhl) *adj.* not able to be corrected

---

1. **smith** (SMITH) *n.* a person who works in metals.

Franklin tells us that he fell short of his goals. Does his attitude about this seem normal to you? Explain.

_____

_____

_____

_____

Read aloud the underlined section. Then, circle the qualities that other people liked in Franklin.

my memory bad, I feel very sensibly the want of it. But, on the whole, though I never arrived at the perfection I had been so ambitious of obtaining, but fell far short of it, yet I was, by the endeavor, a better and a happier man than I otherwise should have been if I had not attempted it.

◆ ◆ ◆

Franklin wants his descendants to know about their ancestor. His list of virtues is important to him. In fact, he says he owes the constant happiness in his life to it. He is now seventy-nine years old. He owes his good health to *Temperance.* He owes his fortune to *Industry* and *Frugality.* To *Sincerity* and *Justice,* he owes the confidence his country has in him.

◆ ◆ ◆

. . . and to the joint influence of the whole mass of the virtues, even in the imperfect state he was able to acquire them, [their ancestor ascribes] all that evenness of temper, and that cheerfulness in conversation, which makes his company still sought for, and agreeable even to his younger acquaintance. I hope, therefore, that some of my descendants may follow the example and reap the benefit.

Vocabulary Development

endeavor (en DEV er) *n.* try, attempt
descendants (dee SEN dents) *n.* people in one's family who come after
ancestor (AN ses ter) *n.* a person in one's family who came before

1. What difficult project does Franklin start?

   _____

2. Franklin makes a list of thirteen items. Each item on the list has two parts. What are those parts?

   1. _____   2. _____

3. Franklin's list has a certain order. He gives the reasons behind that order. On the organizer below, explain the reason for the order of the items.

Temperance is first on the list	because	
Silence is second on the list	because	
Order is third on the list	because	
Resolution is fourth on the list	because	

4. **Reading Strategy:** Franklin tells us that he made a little book. It helped him track his progress with the virtues. What **conclusion** can you **draw** about Franklin's personality, based on this fact?

   _____

   _____

5. **Literary Analysis:** Put a check in front of each of the two sentences that indicate this work is an **autobiography**.

   _____ Franklin is telling the story of his own life.

   _____ Franklin wrote this book when he was seventy-nine.

   _____ Franklin talks about himself, using the pronoun *I*.

   _____ Many people read this book.

   _____ The book has lists in it.

Writing

Autobiographical Account

Write a paragraph about something that has happened in your own life. It might involve your activities, friends, family, or school. Choose an experience that made an impression on you. Tell why the experience was important to you.

1. **Prewriting** Make a list of details about the experience.

   - What happened? _____

   - How did you feel? _____

   - What did you learn? _____

2. **Drafting** Write a draft of your paragraph.

   - As you write, add details that will help your reader understand what happened.

   - Talk about sights, sounds, smells, or anything else that will make your writing more interesting.

   _____

   _____

   _____

   _____

   _____

   _____

3. **Revising** Read your paragraph out loud.

   - Does it sound smooth? If not, maybe you need to add transition words like *first, next, then, because, so,* and *therefore.*

4. **Publishing and Presenting** Write your final paragraph on a separate sheet of paper. Share it with your classmates.

from The Crisis, Number 1
Thomas Paine

Summary

In his essay, Paine encourages the American colonists to fight against the British. He tells his readers that God supports the American cause. Paine says that a good father will fight so that his child may live in peace, and he appeals to all Americans in all states to unite.

Visual Summary

Proposition	Support
All American colonists should fight against the British.	• Britain has declared her right to tax Americans in all cases, and that is tyranny. • Americans have tried to avoid war in every way. • God will not help the British against the Americans because God does not support Britain's tyranny. • A separation from Britain must occur at some point, and it is better to have war now so that our children will have peace. • An offensive war is murder, but this war is just. • The king is like a thief and must be treated the way a thief would be treated.
Conclusion	All Americans should support and participate in the war against the British.

LITERARY ANALYSIS

Persuasion

Persuasion is writing that has these qualities:
- It tries to convince readers to think in a certain way.
- It appeals to emotions or reason or both.
- It gives the writer's opinion.
- It urges action.

In "The Crisis," Thomas Paine tries to persuade the American colonists to fight for freedom from Britain's control. In this passage from the essay, he uses words that appeal to reason and to the emotions:

> These are the times that try men's souls. The summer soldier and the sunshine patriot will in this crisis, shrink from the service of his country; but he that stands it now, deserves the love and thanks of man and woman. Tyranny, like hell, is not easily conquered; yet we have this consolation with us, that the harder the conflict, the more glorious the triumph.

READING STRATEGY

Recognizing Charged Words

Words that get your emotions worked up are called **charged words**. A writer who is trying to persuade is likely to use charged words. These words will get the reader to agree with the writer's point of view. Paine uses many charged words in his essay. As you read, look for some of his charged words. Write them in this chart, and then explain what they mean.

Charged Word	What It Means
EX: tyranny	strong, unfair power over another

from The Crisis

Thomas Paine

Paine says that these are difficult times. He says that those who fight against the British deserve thanks from everyone. He knows that the summer soldier and sunshine patriot[1] will not serve their country in this crisis.

◆　◆　◆

Tyranny, like hell, is not easily conquered; yet we have this consolation with us, that the harder the conflict, the more glorious the triumph. What we obtain too cheap, we esteem too lightly; 'tis dearness only that gives everything its value. Heaven knows how to put a proper price upon its goods.

◆　◆　◆

Paine goes on to say that Britain has a big army to stand behind her tyranny. She has said that she will keep on taxing the colonists and controlling them. Paine says this sounds like slavery. Britain has great power over America. Such power can belong only to God.

Paine believes that God Almighty will not give up on America. That is because America has tried so hard to avoid war. God would not give America up to the care of the devils. Paine says that the king of Britain is like a common murderer or a robber. He has no grounds to look up to heaven for help against America.

◆　◆　◆

Vocabulary Development

tyranny (TEER uh nee) *n.* oppressive or unfair power
consolation (kon suh LAY shuhn) *n.* comfort
esteem (es TEEM) *v.* value

---

1. **summer soldier and sunshine patriot** those who fight only when winning and those who are loyal only during good times.

◆ Reading Strategy

Paine uses **charged words** and phrases in the paragraph. Circle two that are positive. Underline four that are negative.

◆ Literary Analysis

Paine uses facts and emotion to **persuade**, or try to convince his reader to agree with him. List four facts in the bracketed paragraph.

1. _____
2. _____
3. _____
4. _____

I once felt all that kind of anger, which a man ought to feel, against the mean principles that are held by the Tories;[2] a noted one, who kept a tavern at Amboy, was standing at his door, with as pretty a child in his hand, about eight or nine years old, as I ever saw, and after speaking his mind as freely as he thought was <u>prudent</u>, finished with this unfatherly expression, *"Well! give me peace in my day."*

◆ ◆ ◆

Paine says that a <u>generous parent should have said, *"If there must be a war, let it be in my day. That way, my child can have peace."*</u> America could be the happiest place on earth. She is located far from all the <u>wrangling</u> world. All she has to do is trade with the other countries. Paine is sure that America will not be happy until she gets clear of foreign control. Wars, with no endings, will break out until that time comes. America must be the winner in the end.

Paine appeals to Americans in all states to unite. He says that there cannot be too much strength for such an important mission. He wants those in the future to know that when danger arrived, the Americans came together to fight.

Paine explains that British control will affect them all, no matter who they are or where they live.

◆ ◆ ◆

◆ **Stop to Reflect**

Read the underlined sentences. Do you agree with Paine's view here? Why, or why not?

_____

_____

_____

◆ **Reading Check**

What will happen until America wins her freedom? Circle the sentence that answers this question.

Vocabulary Development

prudent (PROO duhnt) *adj.* wise
wrangling (RANG ling) *n.* fighting, bickering, arguing

---

2. **Tories** colonists who were loyal to Britain.

The heart that feels not now, is dead: the blood of his children will curse his <u>cowardice</u>, who shrinks back at a time when a little might have saved the whole, and made *them* happy. (I love the man that can smile at trouble; that can gather strength from distress, and grow brave by reflection.)

◆   ◆   ◆

Paine says that only those with little minds will shrink back. The strong of heart will fight unto death. He would not support an offensive war for all the treasures in the world. Such a war is murder. Paine then asks an important question.

He wonders what is the difference between a thief breaking into his house and ordering him to obey and a king who orders him to obey. He finds no difference and feels that both deserve the same treatment.

◆   ◆   ◆

Vocabulary Development

cowardice (KOW uhr dis) *n.* lack of courage

1. Check the answer that completes the sentence.

    Paine compares tyranny to _____ because it is not easily conquered.

    _____ Great Britain

    _____ summer soldiers

    _____ hell

    _____ heaven

2. On the line, write the answer that best completes the sentence. Choose from the answers in the box.

the Tories are	parents are	children are	God is

    Paine believes that America will win because _____ on America's side.

3. Paine tells of seeing a tavern-keeper in Amboy. The man had a child of eight or nine years old. The man said something that made Paine angry. What did the man say?

    _____

4. Why did Paine get angry at what the man in Amboy said?

    _____

    _____

5. **Literary Analysis:** In your own words, what is Paine trying to **persuade** his readers to do?

    _____

    _____

6. **Reading Strategy:** Circle the one word in each row that could best be called a **charged word**.

glorious	satisfying
control	tyranny
Britain	devils
curse	regret

Listening and Speaking

News Report

With a small group, talk about how a news reporter of the day might have commented on Paine's words. Before your group discussion, write brief answers to these questions:

Who? _____

_____

What? _____

_____

When? _____

_____

Where? _____

_____

Why? _____

_____

When it is your turn to speak, refer to your notes for ideas.

Speech in the Virginia Convention
Patrick Henry

Summary

In this speech, Patrick Henry begins by saying that, without disrespect, he must disagree with the previous speeches. Judging by their conduct, he says, the British are preparing for war. We have tried discussing the problem. We are being ignored; there is no retreat except into slavery. The time for getting along peacefully is over. The war has already begun. "Give me liberty or give me death" is Henry's strong and well-known closing.

Visual Summary

MAIN IDEA

War against the British must happen.

The previous speakers are able and patriotic.	We can only judge the future by the past.	Some say we are too weak to fight the British.
But different men see things differently.	The British have received the petition with a smile.	When will we be stronger?
The question being considered is very important.	But the British are sending fleets and armies to America.	We have three million people to be armed in a just cause.
The debate needs to be free.	We have done everything we can to avoid war.	God will find us friends to fight with us.

LITERARY ANALYSIS

SPEECHES

Speeches are often written first and then delivered orally. A good speaker does these things:

- Uses **restatement**, or restates ideas in a variety of ways
- Uses **repetition**, or repeats ideas using the same words
- Uses **parallelism**, or repeats words and grammatical structure
- Asks **rhetorical questions**, or questions that have obvious answers

In "Speech in the Virginia Convention," Patrick Henry uses all these techniques. Here is an example of his use of rhetorical questions:

> They tell us, sir, that we are weak. . . . But when shall we be stronger? Will it be the next week, or the next year? Will it be when we are totally disarmed, and when a British guard shall be stationed in every house?

READING STRATEGY

Evaluating Persuasive Appeals

When you read a persuasive speech, **evaluate** the **persuasive appeals** being made. Ask yourself if the speaker is appealing to your emotions or to your mind or reason. Use this chart to keep track of phrases and sentences that appeal to the emotions and to reason.

Appeals to Emotions	Appeals to Reason
EX: "nothing less than a question of freedom or slavery"	EX: "different men often see the same subject in different lights"

Speech in the Virginia Convention
Patrick Henry

Mr. President: No man thinks more highly than I do of the patriotism, as well as abilities, of the very worthy gentlemen who have just addressed the house. But different men often see the same subject in different lights. . . .

◆   ◆   ◆

Patrick Henry then says the question before the house is very important. He cannot allow fear of offending someone to stop him from saying what he thinks.

He says it is natural for people to hold on to hope. But no matter how much it hurts, it's best to know the worst and to plan for it.

◆   ◆   ◆

I have but one lamp by which my feet are guided, and that is the lamp of experience. I know of no way of judging of the future but by the past. And judging by the past, I wish to know what there has been in the conduct of the British ministry for the last ten years to justify those hopes with which gentlemen have been pleased to <u>solace</u> themselves and the house? Is it that <u>insidious</u> smile with which our petition has been lately received? Trust it not, sir; it will prove a <u>snare</u> to your feet. Suffer not yourselves to be betrayed with a kiss.[1]

◆   ◆   ◆

---

1. **betrayed with a kiss** In the Bible, Judas betrays Jesus with a kiss. This is a signal to the people who want to arrest Jesus.

◆ **Stop to Reflect**

Do you agree that it is best to know the worst? Why, or why not?

_____

_____

_____

◆ **Read Fluently**

Read aloud the underlined sentences. Then circle the words that tell how Patrick Henry judges the future.

He then says that the British are using the tools of war. What else can the display of British force mean? Does Britain have any enemies in this area of the world? No, she has none. So the navies and armies are here for one reason only.

◆　◆　◆

They are meant for us: they can be meant for no other. They are sent over to bind and rivet upon us those chains which the British ministry have been so long forging.

And what have we to oppose to them? Shall we try argument? Sir, we have been trying that for the last ten years. Have we anything new to offer upon the subject? Nothing. We have held the subject up in every light of which it is capable; but it has been all in vain.

◆　◆　◆

Henry says that the colonists' petitions have been ignored. Their protests have met more violence. Their pleas have been set aside. They have been insulted from the foot of the throne.

◆　◆　◆

There is no longer any room for hope. If we wish to be free, if we mean to preserve inviolate those inestimable privileges for which we have been so long contending, if we mean not basely to abandon the noble struggle in which we have been so long engaged, and which we have pledged ourselves never to abandon until the glorious object of our contest shall be obtained—we must fight! I repeat it, sir, we must fight! An appeal to arms and the God of Hosts is all that is left us!

They tell us, sir, that we are weak—unable to cope with so <u>formidable</u> an <u>adversary</u>. But

---

Vocabulary Development

formidable (FOR mi duh buhl) *adj.*　inspiring fear or awe

adversary (AD ver sair ee) *n.*　enemy, opponent

◆ **Reading Strategy**

Reread the bracketed passage. Then, to **evaluate** Patrick Henry's **persuasive appeals**, check the answer that best completes the sentence.

When Patrick Henry refers to "those chains" that the British have been "forging," he wants his listeners to think that _____.

_____ the British want the colonists to buy new chains from them

_____ the British have put a new tax on chains

_____ the British want to treat the colonists like slaves

_____ the British want the colonists to make more chains

◆ **Reading Check**

Underline the three sentences that tell how the colonists have been treated by Britain.

◆ **Literary Analysis**

Underline the three **rhetorical questions** in the bracketed paragraph here and on page 54. Remember that a rhetorical question is one that has an obvious answer. What are the obvious answers to these questions?

question 1: _____

question 2: _____

question 3: _____

when shall we be stronger? Will it be the next week, or the next year? Will it be when we are totally disarmed, and when a British guard shall be stationed in every house?

◆ ◆ ◆

He continues by saying that the colonists are not weak. There are three million of them. They are "armed in the holy cause of liberty." They cannot be beaten by any force the enemy might send.

◆ ◆ ◆

The battle, sir, is not to the strong alone; it is to the vigilant, the active, the brave. Besides, sir, we have no election; if we were base enough to desire it, it is now too late to retire from the contest. There is no retreat but in submission and slavery! Our chains are forged! Their clanging may be heard on the plains of Boston! The war is inevitable—and let it come! I repeat it, sir, let it come!

It is vain, sir, to extenuate the matter. Gentlemen may cry "Peace, peace"—but there is no peace. The war is actually begun! The next gale that sweeps from the north will bring to our ears the clash of resounding arms! Our brethren are already in the field! Why stand we here idle? What is it that gentlemen wish? What would they have? Is life so dear, or peace so sweet, as to be purchased at the price of chains and slavery? Forbid it, Almighty God! I know not what course others may take; but as for me, give me liberty or give me death!

Vocabulary Development

vigilant (VIJ uh luhnt) *adj.* watchful, alert

extenuate (ex TEN yoo ayt) *v.* to try to lessen how serious something is

◆ Literary Analysis

Henry tells us that the battle is "not to the strong alone." Then he uses **parallelism** to tell us who will fight the battle.

1. What three phrases tell who will fight the battle?

_____

_____

_____

2. Later in this paragraph Henry uses **repetition**. What phrase does he repeat twice?

_____

_____

_____

◆ Reading Strategy

Evaluate the **persuasive appeals** made by Patrick Henry in the last paragraph.

1. How does this paragraph make you feel?

_____

2. Which sentences or phrases make you feel this way? Underline the three sentences or phrases that seem the most powerful to you. Number them 1, 2, 3 in the order of their importance to you.

REVIEW AND ASSESS

1. What does Patrick Henry use to judge what will happen in the future? He states his answer in two ways that mean the same thing. What are they?

   1. _____   2. _____

2. Patrick Henry talks about the navies and armies that Britain has sent to the colonies. Why does he think they are here?

   _____

3. How has Britain responded to the colonists' petitions?

   _____

   _____

4. **Literary Analysis:** Give one example of each of these techniques used in Patrick Henry's speech: **restatement, repetition, parallelism,** and **rhetorical questions.**

   restatement:

   _____

   repetition:

   _____

   parallelism:

   _____

   rhetorical questions:

   _____

5. **Reading Strategy:** Evaluate the **persuasive appeal** of the sentences below by circling the one that is more powerful.

   There is no retreat but in submission and slavery!

   It is now too late to retire from the contest.

Writing

Write Comments on a Speech

Find a written version of a modern speech that you like, such as the Inaugural Speech of John Fitzgerald Kennedy or the Nobel Prize Acceptance Speech of William Faulkner.

Write your comments on the speech. As you write, give your ideas on how well the speaker leads the audience to agree with his or her ideas.

Follow these steps:

1. **Prewriting** Make a bulleted list of the key points in the speech.

    - _____

    - _____

    - _____

    - _____

2. **Drafting** For each point, write a note that tells how the speaker develops that point. In your note, consider these questions:

    (a) Is the point developed through restatement, repetition, parallelism, or rhetorical question?

    _____

    (b) Is the point developed through an appeal to the emotions?

    _____

    (c) Is the point developed through an appeal to reason?

    _____

3. **Revising** Find an example from the speech to prove each point in your draft. Write the example next to your point.

4. **Publishing and Presenting** Compare your comments to the comments of your classmates about the same speech.

Letter to Her Daughter From the New White House

Abigail Adams

Summary

In this selection, Abigail Adams describes her journey to Washington as First Lady. Washington is a new city, with just a few public buildings. The White House is huge, but there are no bells to ring for the thirty servants and there is very little firewood. Adams tells her daughter to tell others that she finds the house and city beautiful. She closes by saying that Mrs. Washington has just invited her to visit Mount Vernon.

Visual Summary

Topic
Life in the new city of Washington

↓

Details						
woods until you reach city	river can be seen from window	grand house but no bells for servants	not enough firewood	six comfortable rooms	oval room very handsome	invitation from Mrs. Washington

↓

Main Idea Sentence
It is a beautiful spot, capable of every improvement, and, the more I view it, the more I am delighted with it.

PRIVATE LETTERS

Private letters are—

- Spontaneous: they are written without being planned.
- Conversational: they sound like everyday speech.
- Private: they are meant to be read only by the person or persons to whom they are written.
- Primary source documents: they reveal information about the time in which they are written.

READING STRATEGY

Distinguishing Between Fact and Opinion

A **fact** is something that can be proved.

An **opinion** is a personal belief that cannot be proved.

When you are judging literary works, it is important to **distinguish between fact and opinion**. Use a chart like this to keep track of facts and opinions in this letter. If you can complete the box under "Yes," then you know the statement is a fact. If you can complete the box under "No," then you know it is an opinion.

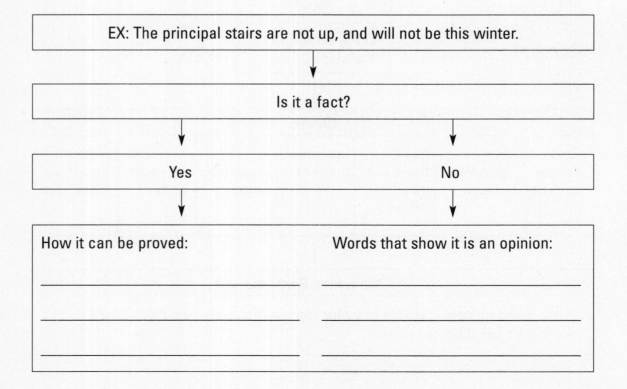

Letter to Her Daughter from the New White House

Abigail Adams

Washington, 21 November, 1800

My Dear Child:

◆　◆　◆

Abigail Adams opens her letter by saying that she got to Washington on Sunday without accidents. But they did get lost outside of Baltimore. Adams says that woods are all you can see from Baltimore until you reach Washington. Here and there you see a small cottage, but you might travel miles without seeing a human being.

◆　◆　◆

In the city there are buildings enough, if they were <u>compact</u> and finished, to <u>accommodate</u> Congress and those attached to it; but as they are, and scattered as they are, I see no great comfort for them. The river,[1] which runs up to Alexandria,[2] is in full view of my window, and I see the vessels as they pass and repass. The house is upon a grand and superb scale, requiring about thirty servants to attend and keep the apartments in proper order, and perform the ordinary business of the house and stables; an establishment very well proportioned to the President's salary.

◆　◆　◆

Vocabulary Development

compact (KAHM pakt) *adj.* close together

accommodate (uh KAHM uh dayt) *v.* to provide with places to live

---

1. **river** the Potomac River, which runs through Washington, D.C.
2. **Alexandria** (al ex AN dree uh) a city in northeastern Virginia.

_____

(2) Do you think those visits were short or long?

_____

(3) Explain your reasoning.

_____

_____

◆ Read Fluently

Read this paragraph aloud. Then circle the answer to this question:

Why isn't wood available for fires?

◆ Literary Analysis

When you read the underlined sentence, you know that this is a **private letter**. How do you know? Give two reasons.

_____

_____

_____

◆ Reading Check

What were the two possible ways of heating the White House in those days?

_____ and _____

Adams goes on to say that the lighting of the apartments is a very difficult job. They also have to keep fires going to keep them from shivering. There are no bells anywhere in the building for calling the servants. Many of the ladies from Georgetown[3] and the city have visited her. Yesterday she returned <u>fifteen visits.</u> She starts to say something about Georgetown but doesn't finish her thought. Instead, she says "our Milton[4] is beautiful."

◆ ◆ ◆

But no comparisons—if they will put me up some bells and let me have wood enough to keep fires, I <u>design</u> to be pleased. I could content myself almost anywhere three months; but, surrounded with forests, can you believe that wood is not to be had because people cannot be found to cut and cart it?

◆ ◆ ◆

She then explains that Briesler was able to get only a few cords of wood. Most of that was used to dry the walls of the house before she and the President got there. Now they have to use coals instead, but they cannot get any grates for the coal.

◆ ◆ ◆

We have, indeed, come into a *new country*. <u>You must keep all this to yourself, and, when asked how I like it, say that I write you the situation is beautiful, which is true.</u> The house is made <u>habitable</u>, but there is not a single

Vocabulary Development

design (dee ZĪN) *v.* intend, plan
habitable (HAB it uh buhl) *adj.* able to be lived in

---

3. **Georgetown** (JAWRJ town): a section of Washington, D.C.
4. **Milton** (MIL tuhn): a town in eastern Massachusetts, south of Boston.

apartment finished, and all withinside,[5] except the plastering, has been done since Briesler came. We have not the least fence, yard, or other convenience without[6] and the great unfinished audience room I make a drying-room of, to hang up the clothes in. The principal stairs are not up, and will not be this winter.

◆ ◆ ◆

Six rooms are comfortable. Two are used by the President and Mr. Shaw. For the past twelve years, this house has been considered as the future headquarters of government. If it had been located in New England, it would have been fixed by now.

◆ ◆ ◆

It is a beautiful spot, capable of every improvement, and, the more I view it, the more I am delighted with it.

Since I sat down to write, I have been called down to a servant from Mount Vernon, with a billet from Major Custis, and a haunch of venison[7], and a kind, congratulatory letter from Mrs. Lewis, upon my arrival in the city, with Mrs. Washington's love, inviting me to Mount Vernon,[8] where, health permitting, I will go before I leave this place.

Affectionately, your mother,

Abigail Adams

◆ **Reading Strategy**

Is the underlined sentence a **fact** or an **opinion**? How do you know? Give one good reason.

_____

_____

_____

Vocabulary Development

billet (BIL uht) *n.* a short letter, a note

---

5. **withinside** (with IN sīd) an old-fashioned way of saying "inside" or "indoors".
6. **without** (with OUT) an old-fashioned way of saying "outside".
7. **haunch of venison** (HAWNCH uv VEN uh suhn) *n.* a large piece of deer meat; half of the back side of a deer.
8. **Mount Vernon** (MOWNT VER nuhn) the estate in Virginia where George and Martha Washington lived.

1. Check the answer that best completes the sentence.

    In 1800, the area between Baltimore and Washington, D.C., was mostly filled with _____.

    ____ little cottages

    ____ woods

    ____ rivers

    ____ buildings with glass windows

2. Complete this sentence by writing the correct word in each blank.

    According to Adams, the two biggest problems in the White House were how to _____ it and how to _____ it.

3. Where does Abigail Adams dry the family's laundry?

    _____

4. Abigail Adams tells her daughter that she has been invited for a visit. Who has invited her, and where has she been invited?

    Who: _____

    Where: _____

5. **Literary Analysis:** As a **primary source document**, this **private letter** gives Adams's view of the White House. Complete this chart listing things Adams says about the new White House. Write three good things and three bad things.

Good Things	Bad Things

6. **Reading Strategy:** Read each phrase or sentence below. Then **distinguish between fact and opinion.** Write *fact* or *opinion* on the line.

1. They went eight or nine miles out of their way on the Frederick road. _____

2. It's a city in name only. _____

3. Wood is not to be had because people cannot be found to cut and cart it. _____

4. It is a beautiful spot, capable of every improvement. _____

Writing

Interview an New Arrival

Interview someone who recently came to this country to live. Find out why and how this person came here. Follow these steps:

- Write a list of questions to ask during the interview.

    1. _____

    2. _____

    3. _____

    4. _____

    5. _____

- Set up a tape recorder to record the interview.

- Make an appointment for your interview.

- During the interview, ask the questions that are on your list.

- Then ask more questions, depending on the person's answers to your questions.

- Take photographs of the person if he or she gives you permission.

- Play your tape recording of the interview for the class and show your photographs.

from Letters From an American Farmer

Michel-Guillaume Jean de Crèvecoeur

Summary

Crèvecoeur describes the opportunities for American immigrants. In Europe, these people are starving and unemployed, but the protective laws of the new land of America help people work and do well. Europeans from all nations come together in America, where all people can work for their own self-interest. Free from dependence and hunger, they can start a new life.

Visual Summary

Topic
Opportunities in America

Europe	America
poverty and starvation	food and opportunity
severe laws	protective laws
no citizenship	citizenship
no ownership of land	potential to own land
the frowns of the rich	rank
no attachment to the country	love of America

LITERARY ANALYSIS

Public Letters

Public letters are—

- Essays written in letter form. They are also called **epistles**.
- Intended for a wide audience.
- **Primary source documents.** This means that they reveal information about the time in which they are written.

READING STRATEGY

Distinguishing Between Fact and Opinion

A **fact** is something that can be proved.

An **opinion** is a personal belief that cannot be proved.

When you are judging literary works, it is important to **distinguish between fact and opinion.** Use this chart to keep track of facts and opinions in this letter. Write facts in the first column. Write opinions in the second column.

Facts	Opinions
EX: The poor of Europe have come to America.	EX: Without owning land, a person can't call a place his country.

from Letters from an American Farmer

Michel-Guillaume Jean de Crèvecoeur

◆ **Literary Analysis**

This **epistle**, or public letter, is a **primary source document**. It tells us about the time in which it was written. What does this paragraph tell you about living conditions for the poor in England at the time? List three facts that are suggested here.

1. _____

   _____

2. _____

   _____

3. _____

   _____

◆ **Reading Check**

To what natural object does Crèvecoeur compare the people who have left Europe?

_____

_____

_____

Crèvecoeur opens by saying that the poor of Europe have come to America for various reasons. He says that two thirds of them had no country. He explains it in this way.

◆　　◆　　◆

Can a wretch who wanders about, who works and starves, whose life is a continual scene of sore <u>affliction</u> or pinching <u>penury</u>, can that man call England or any other kingdom his country? A country that had no bread for him, whose fields <u>procured</u> him no harvest, who met with nothing but the frowns of the rich, the severity of the laws, with jails and punishments; who owned not a single foot of the extensive surface of this planet? No! Urged by a variety of motives, here they came.

◆　　◆　　◆

He goes on to say that everything in America has been better for the poor. In Europe they were like useless plants, in need of rich soil and cool rains. They dried up. They were mowed down by poverty, hunger, and war. Now they have been transplanted here. They have taken root and done well. Here, they are citizens. The laws and their hard work have done it.

◆　　◆　　◆

What attachment can a poor European emigrant have for a country where he had

---

Vocabulary Development

affliction (uh FLIK shuhn) *n.*　terrible troubles, state of distress

penury (PEN yuh ree) *n.*　extreme poverty

procured (proh KYOORD) *v.*　got, obtained

---

nothing? The knowledge of the language, the love of a few kindred as poor as himself, were the only cords that tied him; his country is now that which gives him land, bread, protection, and <u>consequence</u>: *Ubi panis ibi patria*[1] is the motto of all emigrants. What then is the American, this new man? He is either a European, or the descendant of a European, hence that strange mixture of blood, which you find in no other country. I could point out to you a family whose grandfather was an Englishman, whose wife was Dutch, whose son married a French woman, and whose present four sons have now four wives of different nations. *He* is an American, who, leaving behind him all his ancient prejudices and manners, receives new ones from the new mode of life he has embraced, the new government he obeys, and the new rank he holds.

◆ ◆ ◆

Crèvecoeur goes on to say that the emigrant becomes an American by being received into America's broad lap. Here, persons from all nations are melted into a new race of people. The Americans came from all over Europe, and now they live together under the finest system that has ever appeared.

◆ ◆ ◆

<u>The American ought therefore love this country much better than that wherein either he or his forefathers were born</u>. Here the rewards of his industry follow with equal steps

Vocabulary Development

consequence (KAHN suh kwens) *n.* social importance

---

1. *Ubi panis ibi patria* (OO bee PAH nis IB ee PAH tree uh) Latin for "Where there is bread, there is one's fatherland."

_____

_____

_____

_____

What do you think of the definition of an American in the last paragraph?

_____

_____

_____

_____

the progress of his labor; his labor is founded on the basis of nature, *self-interest*; can it want a stronger <u>allurement</u>? Wives and children, who before in vain demanded of him a morsel of bread, now, fat and <u>frolicsome</u>, gladly help their father to clear those fields whence <u>exuberant</u> crops are to arise to feed and to clothe them all.

◆　◆　◆

In America, the farmer does not have to pay large parts of his crop to any princes, abbots,[2] or lords. Here, religion demands little from him. All he has to do is give a small salary to the minister and thanks to God.

◆　◆　◆

The American is a new man, who acts upon new principles; he must therefore entertain new ideas, and form new opinions. From involuntary idleness, servile dependence, penury, and useless labor, he has passed to toils of a very different nature, rewarded by ample <u>subsistence</u>—This is an American.

Vocabulary Development

allurement (uh LOOR muhnt) *n.*　attraction, charm
frolicsome (FRAH lik suhm) *adj.*　full of fun
exuberant (ex OO buhr uhnt) *adj.*　extreme in amount
subsistence (sub SIS tuhns) *n.*　the means to obtain food, shelter, and clothing

---

2. **abbots** (A buhts) heads of small religious groups.

1. How does Crèvecoeur describe the life of the poor European? List three examples.

   1. _____

   2. _____

   3. _____

2. According to Crèvecoeur, what are the advantages of living in America? List them on this graphic organizer.

3. **Literary Analysis:** Suppose Crèvecoeur wrote a **private letter** on the same subject as this **public letter**, or **epistle**. Put a check by each of the phrases below that would appear in a private letter but not in an epistle.

   ____ the new American

   ____ you won't believe this, but

   ____ the rewards of his industry

   ____ don't tell anyone I said this, but

   ____ hope to see you soon

   ____ a new way of living

   ____ acts upon new principles

from Letters from an American Farmer **69**

4. **Reading Strategy:** Crèvecoeur says that in America, everything has been better for the people who came here from Europe. This is his **opinion**. Name at least two **facts** that he uses to support his opinion.

1. _____

2. _____

Writing

Public Letter, or Epistle

Write a **public letter,** or **epistle**, about life in modern America. Imagine that you are writing to people who live in another country. You want them to understand your world. Follow these steps:

1. Think about your audience.

   • To which country are you writing your letter? _____

   • What would be of most interest to your audience? _____

   _____

2. Before you write, limit your topic. You can't write about all aspects of life in America.

   • Pick one aspect to discuss. Write it here: _____

   _____

3. On a separate sheet of paper, write a rough draft of your epistle. Include enough details for your readers to understand your points.

4. Read your letter over to yourself. Imagine that you are a person from the other country.

   • What questions might you want to ask? Write them here: _____

   _____

5. Add any information that would answer those questions and improve your letter.

6. Share your letter with your classmates.

The Devil and Tom Walker
Washington Irving

Summary

Tom Walker meets the Devil ("Old Scratch") in a swamp in thick woods. The Devil offers the pirate Captain Kidd's treasure to Tom on certain conditions. Tom's wife encourages him to accept, but Tom refuses. She leaves to find the Devil and make her own bargain. After her second try, when she takes all the valuable items in the house with her, she doesn't come back. Later, Tom finds her apron with a heart and liver in it. He assumes that the Devil has killed her. Almost grateful, Tom looks for the Devil again. This time, he makes a deal. Tom will get Captain Kidd's treasure if he becomes a moneylender. Later, Tom regrets his deal and starts going to church often. But the Devil returns and sends Tom off on horseback into a storm. Tom never comes back, though his troubled spirit appears on stormy nights.

Visual Summary

Problem	The Devil wants Tom Walker to sell his soul to him.

Event 1: Tom Walker takes a shortcut through the swamp and finds a skull.
Event 2: When he kicks the skull, a stranger shouts at him. The stranger turns out to be the Devil.
Event 3: The Devil offers Tom treasure buried by the pirate Captain Kidd—with conditions.
Event 4: Tom tells his wife about the Devil's offer. His wife wants Tom to accept, but Tom refuses.
Event 5: His wife leaves to bargain with the Devil herself, but she cannot come to terms with him.
Event 6: The next day Tom's wife goes back to meet the Devil, carrying all the valuables from their home.
Event 7: Tom's wife disappears. Tom finds her apron with a heart and liver tied up in it.
Event 8: Now Tom decides to accept the Devil's offer. He agrees to become a moneylender.
Event 9: Tom sets himself up in Boston and loans money at high interest rates. He becomes rich.
Event 10: As he gets older, Tom begins going to church and always carries his Bible with him.

Climax (turning point)
One day Tom steps outside his office—without his Bible—to answer three loud knocks on the door. The Devil has arrived to take his part of the bargain—Tom.

Resolution (conclusion)
Tom is never seen again. But his spirit haunts the swamp.

LITERARY ANALYSIS

Third-Person Omniscient Point of View

Every story has a narrator, or a storyteller. The narrator tells the story from a particular point of view. In the **third-person point of view**, the narrator stands outside the action and is not usually a story character. The third-person narrator is sometimes omniscient (om-NISH-uhnt), or "all knowing." An omniscient narrator. . .

- provides the thoughts and experiences of many characters.
- may tell us things that no character could possibly know.
- may make comments about story events and characters.

As you read Irving's story, use this chart to list details that show that the point of view is omniscient.

Different Characters' Thoughts & Experiences	Things No Character Could Know	Comments About Events & Characters

READING STRATEGY

Inferring Cultural Attitudes

Cultural attitudes are the opinions and values of a particular group of people at a particular time. "The Devil and Tom Walker" takes place in colonial America in the 1720s. From the story's details you can **make inferences**, or draw conclusions, about American cultural attitudes at that time. Use a chart like this one to make inferences.

Detail	Cultural Attitude
Oh, I go by various names. . . . I am the wild huntsman in some countries; the black miner in others. In this neighborhood I am known by the name of the black woodsman.	People believed in the Devil and called him by several nicknames.

The Devil and Tom Walker
Washington Irving

Outside Boston, Massachusetts, in about 1727, Tom Walker lives near a swampy forest. Captain Kidd supposedly buried his pirate treasure in this forest. Tom and his wife are very stingy—so stingy that they even cheat each other. One day, Tom takes a shortcut through the forest. At an old fort that Native Americans had once used in fighting the colonists, Tom meets a mysterious stranger. The stranger, who carries an ax on his shoulder, is not Native American or African American, but he is still very dark, as if covered in soot.

◆ ◆ ◆

"What are you doing on my grounds?" said the black man, with a hoarse growling voice.

"Your grounds!" said Tom with a sneer, "no more your grounds than mine; they belong to Deacon Peabody."

"Deacon Peabody be d____d," said the stranger, "as I flatter myself[1] he will be, if he does not look more to his own sins and less to those of his neighbors. Look yonder, and see how Deacon Peabody is faring."[2]

◆ ◆ ◆

Tom looks at a tree and sees carved into it the name of Deacon Peabody. Deacon Peabody is a local churchman who grew rich through clever land deals. Other trees bear the names of other wealthy members of the community. The trees all have ax marks, and one with the name Crowninshield is completely chopped down.

◆ ◆ ◆

◆ Read Fluently

Read the bracketed passage aloud. Circle the words that show what tones of voice to use.

◆ Reading Check

Irving did not want to spell out "damned," so he wrote "d____d" instead. According to the stranger, why will the deacon be damned? Circle the reason.

---

1. **as I flatter myself** as I am delighted to think.
2. **faring** (FAYR ing) v. doing.

What do you think will happen to Crowninshield? Why?

_____

_____

_____

Circle two nicknames for the Devil that are used by people in Walker's area. From the nicknames, what do you **infer** that European colonists associated with the word *black*? Circle the letter of your answer below.

(a) good   (c) poverty

(b) evil   (d) boldness

An **omniscient**, or all-knowing, **narrator** tells us the thoughts and attitudes of different characters. Circle Tom's wife's thoughts or attitudes about the treasure. Write one word to describe the wife.

_____

"He's just ready for burning!" said the black man, with a growl of triumph. "You see I am likely to have a good stock of firewood for winter."

"But what right have you," said Tom, "to cut down Deacon Peabody's timber?"

"The right of a <u>prior</u> claim," said the other. "This woodland belonged to me long before one of your white-faced race put foot upon the soil."

"And pray, who are you, if I may be so bold?" said Tom.

"Oh, I go by various names. I am the wild huntsman in some countries; the black miner in others. In this neighborhood I am known by the name of the black woodsman. . . . "

"The upshot of all which is, that, if I mistake not," said Tom, sturdily, "you are he commonly called Old Scratch."

"The same, at your service," replied the black man, with a half-civil nod.

◆ ◆ ◆

The Devil offers Tom Captain Kidd's pirate treasure if Tom agrees to his terms. Tom makes no decision. Instead he asks for proof that the Devil is who he says he is. So the Devil presses his finger to Tom's forehead and then goes off. When Tom gets home, he finds a black thumbprint burned into his forehead. He also learns of the sudden death of Absalom Crowninshield. Convinced he has met the Devil, he tells his wife all about it.

◆ ◆ ◆

All her <u>avarice</u> was awakened at the mention of hidden gold, and she urged her husband to <u>comply</u> with the black man's terms and

Vocabulary Development

prior (PRĪ uh) *adj.*   previous; from before

avarice (A vuh riz) *adj.*   greed

comply (kum PLĪ) *v.*   go along with; agree to

secure what would make them wealthy for life. However Tom might have felt disposed to sell himself to the Devil, he was determined not to do so to oblige his wife; so he flatly refused out of the mere spirit of contradiction. Many and bitter were the quarrels they had on the subject, but the more she talked, the more resolute was Tom not to be damned to please her.

At length she determined to drive the bargain on her own account, and if she succeeded, to keep all the gain to herself. Being of the same fearless temper as her husband, she set off for the old Indian fort at the close of a summer's day.

◆ ◆ ◆

To bargain with the Devil, Tom's wife takes the household silverware and other valuables, tying them up in her apron. She is never heard from again. According to one story, Tom goes hunting for her and finds nothing but her apron, with a heart and liver inside! Whatever happened, Tom seems more upset about losing his property than losing his wife. In fact, he decides that the Devil might have done him a favor. Soon he is again bargaining with the Devil to obtain the pirate's treasure.

◆ ◆ ◆

There was one condition which need not be mentioned, being generally understood in all cases where the Devil grants favors; but there were others about which, though of less importance, he was inflexibly obstinate. He

◆ Stop to Reflect

What do you think will happen to Tom's wife?

_____

_____

_____

◆ Stop to Reflect

What "one condition which need not be mentioned" is always involved when someone makes a deal with the Devil? Circle the letter of the correct answer below.

(a) person damned in the after-life

(b) person signs name in blood

(c) person becomes rich

(d) person gets revenge on enemies

Vocabulary Development

secure (se KYOOR) *v.* to make certain about; to guarantee

disposed (dis POHZD) *adj.* inclined; prone to

oblige (u BLĪDG) *v.* do what someone else wants; please

inflexibly (in FLEHKS uh blee) *adv.* completely unwilling to move or change

obstinate (AWB sti net) *adj.* stubborn

From the details in the bracketed paragraph, what can you **infer** about the attitude people in Tom's day had toward slavery?

_____

_____

_____

_____

Do you think Tom will regret his decision? Circle your answer.

  yes   no

Why, or why not?

_____

_____

_____

insisted that money found through his means should be employed in his service. He proposed, therefore, that Tom should employ it in the black traffic; that is to say, that he should fit out a slave ship. This, however, Tom <u>resolutely</u> refused: he was bad enough in all conscience, but the Devil himself could not tempt him to turn slave-trader.

Finding Tom so squeamish on this point, he did not insist upon it, but proposed, instead, that he should turn usurer.[3] . . .

To this no objections were made, for it was just to Tom's taste.

"You shall open a broker's shop[4] in Boston next month," said the black man.

"I'll do it tomorrow, if you wish," said Tom Walker.

"You shall lend money at two per cent a month."

"Egad, I'll charge four!" replied Tom Walker. . . .

"Done!" said the Devil.

"Done!" said Tom Walker. So they shook hands and struck a bargain.

◆ ◆ ◆

So Tom becomes a cruel moneylender, charging his highest rates to his most desperate customers. He grows rich and powerful. He builds a large, showy house, though he is too stingy to furnish it well. He buys a fancy carriage but lets the horses nearly starve. Yet as he nears old age, he begins to worry.

◆ ◆ ◆

Vocabulary Development

resolutely (re zoh LOOT lee) *adv.* firmly

---

3. **usurer** (YOO zer rer) *n.* a moneylender who charges high interest rates.
4. **a broker's shop** a moneylending business.

Having secured the good things of this world, he began to feel anxious about those of the next. He thought with regret on the bargain he had made with his black friend, and set his wits to work to cheat him out of the conditions. He became, therefore, all of a sudden, a violent churchgoer. . . . Tom was as rigid in religious as in money matters; he was a stern supervisor and censurer[5] of his neighbors, and seemed to think every sin entered up to their account became a credit on his own side of the page.

◆ ◆ ◆

Frightened of the Devil, Tom keeps a small Bible in his coat pocket and a large one on his desk at work. One hot afternoon, while still in his bathrobe, Tom sits in his office demanding repayment of a loan. The man who has taken the loan is a land jobber, or speculator, who tried to make money by buying and selling land. In the past, Tom has acted as if this man were a good friend. Now Tom refuses to give him more time to repay his loan.

◆ ◆ ◆

"My family will be ruined and brought upon the parish," said the land jobber.

"Charity begins at home," replied Tom; "I must take care of myself in these hard times."

"You have made so much money out of me," said the speculator.

Tom lost his patience and his <u>piety</u>—"The Devil take me," said he, "if I have made a farthing!"[6]

Vocabulary Development

piety (Pī e tee) *n.* religious devotion

◆ **Reading Check**

As a result of worrying about his deal with the Devil, what does Tom become? Circle your answer.

Why is he so critical of other people's sins? Put a box around the reason.

◆ **Literary Analysis**

What does the **omniscient narrator** think about Tom at this point?

_____

_____

_____

_____

◆ **Stop to Reflect**

Circle the proverb, or saying, Tom uses to defend his behavior here. What is dishonest about his words of defense?

_____

_____

_____

---

5. **censurer** (SEN sher rer) *n.* someone who criticizes the behavior of others.
6. **farthing** (FAHR thing) *n.* a small coin of little value.

Do you think Tom deserves this doom?

_____

_____

Why, or why not?

_____

_____

_____

_____

Circle the sentence in which the **omniscient narrator** gives advice directly to some of his readers. What does he want those readers to learn from the story?

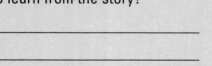

_____

_____

_____

Just then there were three loud knocks at the street door. He stepped out to see who was there. A black man was holding a black horse, which neighed and stamped with impatience.

"Tom, you're come for," said the black fellow, <u>gruffly</u>. Tom shrunk back, but too late. He had left his little Bible at the bottom of his coat pocket, and his big Bible on the desk . . . never was a sinner taken more unawares.

◆ ◆ ◆

The Devil takes Tom up and rides off into a thunderstorm. They are said to have galloped like mad to the swamp by the old fort. Shortly afterward the forest is struck by lightning. The next day Tom's fancy new house catches fire and burns to the ground. Tom himself is never seen again. Those appointed to settle his affairs find nothing but ashes where his business papers should be. They also find chests filled with worthless wood shavings instead of gold.

◆ ◆ ◆

Such was the end of Tom Walker and his ill-gotten wealth. Let all <u>griping</u> money brokers lay this story to heart. The truth of it is not to be doubted. The very hole under the oak trees, whence[7] he dug Kidd's money, is to be seen to this day; and the neighboring swamp and old Indian fort are often haunted in stormy nights by a figure on horseback, in morning gown and white cap, which is doubtless the troubled spirit of the usurer.

Vocabulary Development

gruffly (GRUHF lee) *adv.* abruptly
griping (GRĪP ing) *adj.* complaining

---

7. **whence** (WENS) *prep.* from where.

1. Circle the words that best describe Tom Walker.

    greedy   loyal   loving   selfish   lazy

2. What happens to Tom's wife?

    _____

    _____

3. Complete these sentences to explain the bargain that Tom makes.

    Tom agrees to _____

    in exchange for _____.

4. What happens to Tom in the end?

    _____

    _____

5. **Literary Analysis:** Show that the story uses **third-person omniscient point of view** by finding examples for the chart below.

Different Characters' Thoughts & Experiences:	Comments About Events & Characters:

6. **Reading Strategy:** Put a check in front of each **cultural attitude** that you can **infer** from the details in the story.

_____ Few people of the time believed in the Devil.

_____ Many European colonists distrusted Native Americans.

_____ Most colonists admired pirates and thought they were heroes.

_____ Some people disliked the slave trade.

_____ Some moneylenders charged high interest rates.

_____ Boston was a center of colonial commerce.

_____ The Bible was not an important book in colonial times.

Writing

Modern Story

Imagine that you are updating Irving's story. Your new version will take place in the United States today. Answer these questions about changes you might make in the story.

- Where would Tom meet the Devil?

_____

- How would Tom's wife disappear?

_____

- What treasure would the Devil give Tom?

_____

- What job or career would the Devil choose for Tom?

_____

- What would Tom buy or do when he is rich?

_____

- What would happen at the end?

_____

Now, write the first paragraph of your new story on separate paper. Share it with your classmates and get their reactions.

A Psalm of Life

Henry Wadsworth Longfellow

Summary

In this poem, the speaker refuses to accept the idea that life is only a dream with the grave as its only goal. The soul is eternal. Heroic action in life is important because life is short. The lives of heroes who have gone before us remind us that we, too, can be examples of courage and achievement for others.

Visual Summary

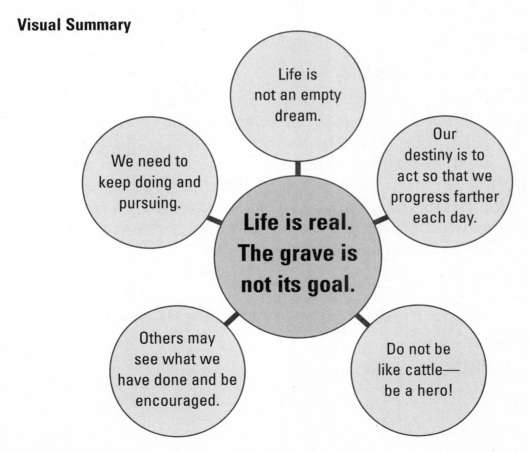

Life is not an empty dream.

We need to keep doing and pursuing.

Our destiny is to act so that we progress farther each day.

Life is real. The grave is not its goal.

Others may see what we have done and be encouraged.

Do not be like cattle— be a hero!

LITERARY ANALYSIS

Stanza Form

Many poems are written in groups of lines called **stanzas**. Each stanza is something like a paragraph, usually focusing on one main idea. A two-line stanza is called a couplet. A four-line stanza is called a quatrain (KWA train). The subject of this **quatrain** from "A Psalm of Life" is human achievement:

> Life is real! Life is earnest!
> > And the grave is not its goal:
> Dust thou art, to dust returnest,
> > Was not spoken of the soul.

Stanzas follow a set pattern of rhythm and rhyme. If you read the above stanza aloud, you can hear the rhythm. Also, the words at the ends of the first and third lines rhyme: *earnest/returnest*. Those at the end of the second and fourth lines rhyme too: *goal/soul*.

As you read "A Psalm of Life," see if the other stanzas follow this pattern. Also think about the main idea of each stanza.

READING STRATEGY

Associating Images with Life

An **image** is something you can see, smell, taste, touch, or hear. Poets often use images that take on greater meaning when we think about them in relation to human life. For example, when Longfellow talks about "the world's broad field of battle," he seems to be comparing life to a large struggle in which each person plays a role. To **associate images with life**, think about what each image means in a larger context. Use this diagram to help you.

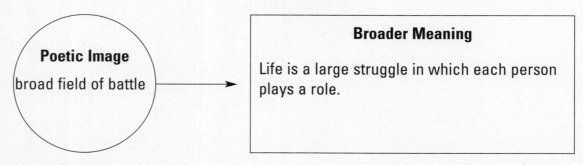

Poetic Image
broad field of battle

Broader Meaning

Life is a large struggle in which each person plays a role.

A Psalm of Life
Henry Wadsworth Longfellow

Tell me not, in mournful numbers,
    Life is but an empty dream!–
For the soul is dead that slumbers,
    And things are not what they seem.

Life is real! Life is earnest!
    And the grave is not its goal:
Dust thou art, to dust returnest,[1]
    Was not spoken of the soul.

◆ ◆ ◆

Happiness and sadness aren't our destiny.
Our destiny is to make progress every day.

◆ ◆ ◆

In the world's broad field of battle,
    In the bivouac[2] of Life,
Be not like dumb, driven cattle!
    Be a hero in the strife!

◆ ◆ ◆

Don't worry about the past or the future.
Act in the present.

◆ ◆ ◆

Lives of great men all remind us
    We can make our lives <u>sublime</u>,
And, departing, leave behind us
    Footprints on the sands of time;

Footprints, that perhaps another,
    Sailing o'er life's solemn main,[3]
A forlorn and shipwrecked brother,
    Seeing, shall take heart again.

◆ ◆ ◆

Let us be active and ready for any fate.

Vocabulary Development

sublime (suh BLĪM) *adj.* noble; inspiring

---

1. **Dust thou art, to dust returnest** You are dust, and you return to dust; a rewording of a famous quotation from the Bible (Genesis 3:19).
2. **bivouac** (BIV wak) *n.* temporary army camp.
3. **o'er life's solemn main** over the sad open sea of life.

◆ **Literary Analysis**

Show the sound pattern in this **stanza** by circling and connecting the rhyming words. What is the stanza's main idea? Circle the letter of the answer below.

(a) Sadness cannot be measured.

(b) Do not give up hope.

(c) The soul is dead.

(d) Everyone needs to take a rest.

◆ **Reading Check**

The speaker tells us not to be like dumb, or silent, cattle driven to market. What does he tell us to be instead? Circle the word.

◆ **Reading Strategy**

Associate the image of the footprints with life. What are the footprints? Circle the letter of the best answer below.

(a) clues

(b) death

(c) human achievements

(d) walks on the beach

1. Circle the word that best describes the speaker's attitude.

   bitter   positive   hopeless   humorous   shy

2. Put a check in front of those ideas with which the speaker agrees.

   ____ Life is but an empty dream!   ____ Life is real!

   ____ The grave is the goal of life.   ____ Life is earnest!

3. What does the speaker think the lives of great men can teach us? Circle the letter of the best answer.

   (a) how to be modest

   (b) how to make money

   (c) how to walk without shoes

   (d) how to be great ourselves

4. **Literary Analysis:** On the chart, list the main idea of each **stanza**.

Stanza	Main Idea
1	
2	
3	
4	
5	

5. **Reading Strategy:** Explain what each **image** below means or says about life in general.

Image	Broad Meaning
to dust returneth	
dumb, driven cattle	
footprints on the sands of time	
shipwrecked brother	

Writing

Comparing Ideas

Choose a proverb or saying from the list below. Then, write a paragraph showing how the ideas of the proverb or saying are similar to those in the poem.

- Put a check next to the one proverb or saying you think has ideas most similar to those in the poem:

____ Make the most of life while you can.

____ It is better to give than to receive.

____ Keep hope alive.

____ We can all make a difference in life.

- In the space below, list similarities between the proverb or saying and the poem.

Proverb or Saying	Poem

- On separate paper, write a paragraph showing how the poem expresses ideas similar to those in the proverb or saying. Include the similarities you listed in the chart.
- Share the paragraph with your classmates. Ask them if they agree with your ideas.

The Raven
Edgar Allan Poe

Summary

In this poem, the speaker is reading at night. A mysterious raven arrives. To all the speaker's questions, the raven says, "Nevermore!" The speaker demands that the raven leave, but it stays, haunting him forever.

Visual Summary

What the speaker of the poem says	What the speaker hears the raven answer
• Excuse me, I was napping.	No response
• Lenore!	No response
• Tell me your name.	"Nevermore."
• The bird will leave me tomorrow, as others have.	"Nevermore."
• I need respite from my grief over Lenore.	"Nevermore."
• "Is there balm in Gilead?"	"Nevermore."
• Will I hold Lenore again?	"Nevermore."
• Leave my door.	"Nevermore."

LITERARY ANALYSIS

Single Effect

Poe believed that a good poem or story should have "a certain unique and **single effect**" on the reader. He thought that all the details should work toward that effect. In most of Poe's poems and stories, the single effect he tried to achieve was horror. To achieve it in "The Raven," for instance, he writes about a large dark bird associated with bad luck. He sets the poem at night. And he uses words like *ghastly* (which means "awful") and *grim* to stress the horror:

> Ghastly grim and ancient Raven wandering from
> the Nightly shore—

As you read "The Raven," look for other details that contribute to the single effect.

READING STRATEGY

Breaking Down Long Sentences

Poems often use long sentences that continue over many lines. To understand what they are saying, it helps to **break down long sentences** into parts and see how those parts are related. To break down a sentence, identify the core of subject, verb, and direct object. Then look for clues in punctuation and connecting words. These clues help you to figure out how all the main chunks are related to the core. Use a diagram like this.

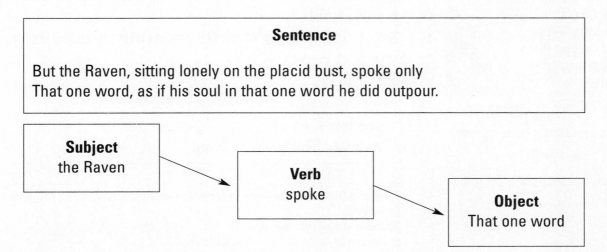

Sentence

But the Raven, sitting lonely on the placid bust, spoke only
That one word, as if his soul in that one word he did outpour.

Subject
the Raven

Verb
spoke

Object
That one word

The Raven
Edgar Allan Poe

Once upon a midnight dreary, while I
    <u>pondered</u>, weak and weary,
Over many a quaint and curious volume of
    forgotten lore[1]—
While I nodded, nearly napping, suddenly there
    came a tapping,
As of some one gently rapping, rapping at my
    chamber door.
"'Tis some visitor," I muttered, "tapping at my
    chamber door—
                    Only this, and nothing more."

Ah, distinctly I remember it was in the bleak
    December;
And each separate dying ember <u>wrought</u> its
    ghost upon the floor.
Eagerly I wished the morrow;[2]—vainly I had
    sought to borrow
From my books surcease[3] of sorrow—sorrow
    for the lost Lenore—
For the rare and radiant maiden whom the
    angels name Lenore—
                    Nameless *here* for evermore.

<u>And the silken, sad, uncertain rustling of each
    purple curtain</u>
Thrilled me—filled me with fantastic terrors
    never felt before;
So that now, to still the beating of my heart, I
    stood repeating

◆ Literary Analysis

Which details about the time of the poem's events help establish the **single effect** of horror? Circle two details in these bracketed lines.

◆ Stop to Reflect

What was the speaker's relationship with Lenore, and what probably happened to her?

_____

_____

_____

◆ Read Fluently

Read the underlined line aloud. Circle the four /*s*/ sounds. What sound do you think Poe is trying to capture?

(a) the curtains rustling

(b) the speaker's beating heart

(c) the speaker's terror

(d) a visitor knocking on the door

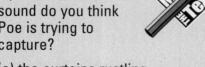

Vocabulary Development

pondered (PAHN duhrd) *v.* thought deeply
wrought (RAWT) *v.* carved

---

1. **quaint** (KWAYNT) **volume of forgotten lore** unusual book of forgotten knowledge.
2. **the morrow** the next day.
3. **surcease** (suhr SEES) **of** Relief from.

"'Tis some visitor entreating entrance at my
   chamber door—
Some late visitor entreating entrance at my
   chamber door;—
          This it is and nothing more."

Presently my soul grew stronger; hesitating
   then no longer,
"Sir," said I, "or Madam, truly your forgiveness
   I implore;
But the fact is I was napping, and so gently
   you came rapping,
And so faintly you came tapping, tapping at
   my chamber door,
That I scarce was sure I heard you"—here I
   opened wide the door;—
        Darkness there and nothing more.

        ◆ ◆ ◆

    The speaker searches the dark for the
source of the knocking, but he sees nothing.
When he calls out the name "Lenore," he hears
only an echo. Then hears the knocking again.
This time he thinks it is someone at the window.

        ◆ ◆ ◆

<u>Open here I flung the shutter,</u> when, with
   many a flirt and flutter,
In there stepped a <u>stately</u> Raven of the
   saintly days of yore;[4]
Not the least obeisance[5] made he; not a
   minute stopped or stayed he;
But, with mien[6] of lord or lady, perched
   above my chamber door—
Perched upon a bust of Pallas[7] just above my
   chamber door—
       Perched, and sat, and nothing more.

◆ Reading Check

What does the speaker
find when he opens the
door? Circle your answer.

◆ Reading Strategy

Break up the underlined
clause that begins this
long sentence. Circle the
subject of the clause and
label it *S.* Circle the verb
and label it *V.* Circle the
object and label it *O.*

Vocabulary Development

stately (STAYT lee) *adj.* elegant; dignified

---

4. **days of yore** (YAWR) olden days; days of long ago.
5. **obeisance** (oh BAY suhns) *n.* show of respect, such as a bow or a curtsy.
6. **mien** (MEEN) *n.* manner; way of conducting yourself.
7. **bust of Pallas** (PAL is) sculpture of the head and shoulders of Pallas Athena (uh THEE nuh), the ancient Greek goddess of wisdom.

Then this ebony bird beguiling my sad fancy[8]
    into smiling,
By the grave and stern decorum[9] of the
    countenance[10] it wore,
"Though thy crest be shorn and shaven,[11]
    thou," I said, "art sure no <u>craven</u>,
Ghastly grim and ancient Raven wandering
    from the Nightly shore—
Tell me what thy lordly name is on the Night's
    Plutonian[12] shore!"
            Quoth[13] the Raven, "Nevermore."

Much I marveled[14] this <u>ungainly</u> fowl to hear
    discourse[15] so plainly,
Though its answer little meaning—little
    relevancy bore;[16]
For we cannot help agreeing that no living
    human being
Ever yet was blessed with seeing bird above his
    chamber door—
Bird or beast upon the sculptured bust above
    his chamber door,
            With such name as "Nevermore."

◆ Reading Strategy

This stanza is one long sentence. Draw lines between words to **break up the long sentence** into manageable chunks. Circle the letter of the statement below that best sums up the meaning of the sentence.

(a) I was amazed by the bird and its speech, even if it made little sense.

(b) I was amazed that anything so ugly could have such a lovely voice.

(c) I chatted with the amazing bird, which sat on a bust labeled "Nevermore" over my door.

(d) I am the only human being who ever spoke with Nevermore.

Vocabulary Development

craven (KRAYV uhn) *n.* coward
ungainly (uhn GAYN lee) *adj.* awkward; clumsy

---

8. **ebony** (EB uh nee) **bird beguiling** (bi GīL ing) **my sad fancy** black bird charming my sad mood away.
9. **decorum** (duh KAWR uhm) *n.* act of polite behavior.
10. **countenance** (KOW tuh nuns) *n.* face.
11. **thy crest be shorn and shaven** The tuft of feathers on your head is clipped and shaved (by a previous owner).
12. **Plutonian** (ploo TOHN yuhn) *adj.* Dark and evil; hellish (Pluto was the Roman god of the underworld).
13. **quoth** (KWOHTH) *v.* quoted; recited; said.
14. **marveled** found marvelous; felt awe or wonder about.
15. **discourse** (dis KAWRS) *v.* speak; talk.
16. **little relevancy** (REL uh vin see) **bore** had little meaning; did not make much sense.

But the Raven, sitting lonely on the placid[17] bust, spoke only
That one word, as if his soul in that one word he did outpour.
Nothing farther then he uttered—not a feather then he fluttered—
Till I scarcely more than muttered, "Other friends have flown before—
On the morrow *he* will leave me, as my Hopes have flown before."
    <u>Then the bird said, "Nevermore."</u>

◆ ◆ ◆

The speaker worries about this "Nevermore." This time it sounds like a real answer to the question he asked. He tells himself that maybe the Raven knows just this one word. Yet he still keeps trying to find some meaning in the word. No matter what he asks the Raven, the bird says, "Nevermore." By now the speaker is angry.

◆ ◆ ◆

"Prophet!" said I, "thing of evil!—prophet still, if bird or devil!
By that Heaven that bends above us—by that God we both adore—
Tell this soul with sorrow laden[18] if, within the distant Aidenn,[19]
It shall clasp a sainted maiden whom the angels name Lenore—
Clasp a rare and radiant maiden whom the angels name Lenore."
    Quoth the Raven, "Nevermore."

---

17. **placid** (PLA sid) *adj.* silent.
18. **this soul with sorrow laden** (LAY duhn) the speaker's own sorrowful soul.
19. **Aidenn** (AY duhn) Eden; heaven.

◆ **Reading Check**

What does the speaker think the Raven means when he says "Nevermore" in the underlined sentence?

_____

_____

_____

◆ **Literary Analysis**

How does the repetition of "Nevermore" add to the **single effect** of horror? Explain.

_____

_____

_____

Circle two more details on this page that add to the single effect of horror.

"Be that word our sign of parting, bird or
  fiend!" I shrieked, upstarting[20] —
"Get thee back into the tempest and the Night's
  Plutonian shore!
Leave no black plume as a token of that lie thy
  soul hath spoken!
Leave my loneliness unbroken!—quit the bust
  above my door!
Take thy beak from out my heart, and take thy
  form from off my door!"
                    Quoth the Raven, "Nevermore."

And the Raven, never flitting, still is sitting,
  still is sitting
On the pallid bust of Pallas just above my
  chamber door;
And his eyes have all the seeming of a demon's
  that is dreaming;
And the lamp-light o'er him streaming throws
  his shadow on the floor;
And my soul from out that shadow that lies
  floating on the floor
                    Shall be lifted—nevermore!

◆ Reading Check

What is the situation at the end of the poem? Answer by completing this sentence:
The Raven is _____

_____,

and the speaker is _____

_____.

Vocabulary Development

fiend (FEEND) *n.* demon; devil
plume (ploom) *n.* feather
flitting (FLIT ing) *adj.* flying rapidly
pallid (PAL uhd) *adj.* pale; white

---

20. **upstarting** starting up; standing; moving.

REVIEW AND ASSESS

1. Circle the words that best describe the speaker in this poem.

   cruel   sad   brooding   hopeless   boring   superstitious

2. On the line before each statement, write *T* if the statement seems true. Write *F* if it seems false.

   ____ The speaker misses Lenore.

   ____ Lenore is away visiting her parents for the holidays.

   ____ The speaker is reading a book about bird watching.

   ____ The Raven enters through the window.

   ____ The Raven has an extensive vocabulary.

   ____ The Raven perches on a bust of an ancient Greek goddess.

   ____ The Raven is still perched on the bust when the poem ends.

3. List three things that the speaker thinks "Nevermore" may mean.

   • _____

   • _____

   • _____

4. Many people find "The Raven" very musical. Show its music by listing at least four examples of rhyme and other repeated sounds.

   • _____

   • _____

   • _____

   • _____

5. **Literary Analysis:** On the chart below, list details from the poem that contribute to the **single effect** of horror. Include at least two details in each part of the chart.

Setting (time or place)	
Characters	
Events	
Word Choice	

6. **Reading Strategy:** Use lines to **break this sentence** into parts. Underline and label the subject (S), the verb (V), and the object (O).

But the Raven, sitting lonely on the placid bust, spoke only

That one word, as if his soul in that one word he did outpour.

Listening and Speaking

Dramatic Reading

Prepare and present a dramatic reading of one stanza of "The Raven." Follow this procedure:

- Practice reading the stanza in front of a mirror, with friends or family, or on audiocassette or videotape.

- Underline any words that give you trouble, and practice until you get them right.

- Use a dramatic tone that conveys the single effect of horror.

- Use body language to help communicate ideas and feelings.

Present your dramatic reading to your class.

from Walden

Henry David Thoreau

Summary

In this excerpt from *Walden*, Thoreau almost buys a farm. Its attraction is that it is far from its neighbors. But the owner's wife changes her mind, and Thoreau decides it is too much of a commitment. Instead he builds a cabin in the woods, where he wants to deal only with the essentials of life. His cabin is open and airy, allowing him to live in touch with nature. He urges his readers to make their lives simple and not to spend time on useless details. He says that so-called improvements only make our lives more complicated.

Visual Summary

Topic: Living a simple life	
Thoreau's Statement	**Details**
The Hollowell farm has real attractions.	• Far from the village (two miles). • Half a mile from the nearest neighbor and separated from the highway by a field. • Situated on the river, with apple trees gnawed by rabbits.
I went to the woods because I wished to live deliberately.	• Began to spend nights there on Independence Day. • Cabin is airy and unplastered. • Wishes to live deep and to know life by experience.
Simplicity, simplicity, simplicity!	• Keep activities to two or three instead of thousands. • Have one meal a day instead of three. • Be as wise as the day you were born.
I left the woods for as good a reason as I went there.	• He had several more lives to live. • In only a week, he wore a path from his door to the side of the pond.
However mean your life is, meet it and live it....Money is not required to buy one necessary of the soul.	• A faultfinder will find faults even in paradise. • You may have glorious hours even in a poorhouse. • Do not get new things.

LITERARY ANALYSIS

Style

Style is the way in which a writer puts thoughts into words. Every writer has his or her own particular style. Style includes the words the writer chooses and the way he or she joins those words together into sentences and paragraphs. Thoreau's style is known for these elements:

- simple, direct language
- images from nature and everyday life
- sentences of varied length, including occasional short sentences
- figurative language, or language not meant to be taken literally

As you read the selection from *Walden*, look for these four elements of Thoreau's style.

READING STRATEGY

Evaluating the Writer's Philosophy

A writer's **philosophy** is the body of ideas that he or she has about life and how it should be lived. When you read these ideas, you should not accept them without question. Instead, **evaluate the writer's philosophy** by asking these questions:

- Is the idea presented clearly in a way that makes sense?
- Is the idea supported with enough examples and reasons?
- Does the idea match my own knowledge and experience?

As you read this selection from *Walden*, use a diagram like this one to help you evaluate the ideas of Thoreau's philosophy.

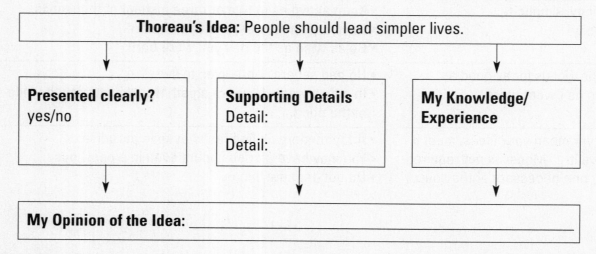

Thoreau's Idea: People should lead simpler lives.

Presented clearly?
yes/no

Supporting Details
Detail:

Detail:

My Knowledge/
Experience

My Opinion of the Idea: _____

from Walden

Henry David Thoreau

When he was twenty-eight, Thoreau decided to leave the village of Concord, Massachusetts. He went to live several miles from town in the woods at Walden Pond. There he built a simple cabin that was little more than a shelter from the rain. He moved in on July 4, 1845—Independence Day. In a section of *Walden* called "Where I Lived and What I Lived For," he explains why he decided to live such a simple, rugged life, close to nature.

◆ ◆ ◆

I went to the woods because I wished to live deliberately, to front[1] only the essential facts of life, and see if I could not learn what it had to teach, and not, when I came to die, discover that I had not lived. I did not wish to live what was not life, living is so dear; nor did I wish to practice resignation, unless it was quite necessary.

◆ ◆ ◆

◆ **Reading Check**

When he went to the woods, what kind of life experiences was Thoreau hoping to face? Circle the answer in the bracketed paragraph.

Thoreau went to the woods because he wanted to live life fully and find out what it was all about. If it was wonderful, he wanted to enjoy it. If it was awful, he wanted to face that too. He feels that too many people don't understand the meaning of life. Instead they live in a small way, like ants.

◆ ◆ ◆

◆ **Stop to Reflect**

How would living in the woods help Thoreau live life more fully?

_____

_____

_____

_____

Vocabulary Development

deliberately (duh LIB rit lee) *adv.* with thought and care

essential (uh SEN shuhl) *adj.* vital; necessary

resignation (re zig NAY shuhn) *n.* giving in to conditions beyond your control; hopelessness

---

1. **front** confront; face.

Our life is <u>frittered away</u> by detail. An honest man has hardly need to count more than his ten fingers, or in extreme cases he may add his ten toes, and lump the rest. <u>Simplicity, simplicity, simplicity!</u> I say, let your affairs be as two or three, and not a hundred or a thousand; instead of a million count half a dozen, and keep your accounts on your thumbnail. In the midst of this chopping sea of civilized life, such are the clouds and storms and quicksands and thousand-and-one items to be allowed for, that a man has to live, if he would not founder[2] and go to the bottom and not make his port at all, by dead reckoning.[3] Simplify, simplify. Instead of three meals a day, if it be necessary eat but one; instead of a hundred dishes, five; and reduce other things in proportion.

◆ ◆ ◆

Thoreau complains that there is too much stress on business and commerce in the young American nation. To him, the focus on material things is shallow. It takes people away from the more important spiritual side of life. Instead of wasting time working on new inventions, like the telegraph and the railroad, Thoreau thinks people should work on their souls. He sees no need to travel farther and faster on the railroad. He thinks people should not be in such a hurry to get nowhere different in their lives.

◆ ◆ ◆

Vocabulary Development

frittered (FRIT uhrd) **away** wasted, bit by bit

---

2. **founder** (FOWN duhr) *v.* fill up with water and sink.
3. **dead reckoning** (REK uhn ing) sailing without using the stars to guide you.

Time is but the stream I go a-fishing in. I drink at it; but while I drink I see the sandy bottom and detect how shallow it is. Its thin current slides away, but eternity remains. I would drink deeper; fish in the sky, whose bottom is pebbly with stars. I cannot count one. I know not the first letter of the alphabet. I have always been regretting that I was not as wise as the day I was born. The intellect is a <u>cleaver</u>; it <u>discerns</u> and rifts[4] its way into the secret of things. I do not wish to be any more busy with my hands than is necessary. <u>My head is hands and feet.</u> I feel all my best <u>faculties</u> concentrated in it.

◆ ◆ ◆

Thoreau explains why he leaves his cabin on Walden Pond and returns to civilization.

◆ ◆ ◆

I left the woods for as good a reason as I went there. Perhaps it seemed to me that I had several more lives to live, and could not spare any more time for that one. It is remarkable how easily and insensibly[5] we fall into a particular route, and make a beaten track for ourselves. I had not lived there a week before my feet wore a path from my door to the pondside; and though it is five or six years since I trod[6] it, it is still quite distinct. It is true, I fear that others may have fallen into it, and so helped to keep it open. The surface of

---

Vocabulary Development

cleaver (KLEE vuhr) *n.* a tool for cutting

discerns (di SERNZ) *v.* recognizes separate ideas

faculties (FAK uhl teez) *n.* powers; abilities

---

4. **rifts** cuts through; divides.
5. **insensibly** (in SEN suh blee) *adv.* without noticing.
6. **trod** walked.

◆ **Literary Analysis**

Thoreau's **style** uses simple word choice, natural or everyday images, figurative language, and some short sentences. What everyday subject provides Thoreau's images in this bracketed passage?

_____

Circle an example of figurative language, and put a box around a short sentence.

◆ **Stop to Reflect**

What does the underlined statement mean? Circle the letter of the best answer below.

(a) It is important to keep busy.

(b) Being disabled need not prevent someone from leading a full life.

(c) Thinking is more important than physical action.

(d) The senses of sight, smell, taste, and hearing are more important than the sense of touch.

◆ **Reading Check**

Why did Thoreau leave the woods? Answer by completing the sentence below.

He left because his life there had become

_____

_____

_____ .

the earth is soft and impressible by the feet of men; and so with the paths which the mind travels. How worn and dusty, then, must be the highways of the world, how deep the ruts of tradition and conformity!

◆　◆　◆

Thoreau explains the things he learned from living in the woods. First, if a person follows his or her dreams, he or she will be rewarded in unexpected ways. Second, the more simply a person lives, the more rewarding his or her life will be. And last, there is no need to try to be like everyone else.

◆　◆　◆

Why should we be in such desperate <u>haste</u> to succeed, and in such desperate <u>enterprises</u>? If a man does not keep <u>pace</u> with his companions, perhaps it is because he hears a different drummer. Let him step to the music which he hears, however measured[7] or far away.

◆　◆　◆

To Thoreau, being alone is not the same as being lonely. And being poor does not stop you from enjoying the important things in life.

◆　◆　◆

<u>However <u>mean</u> your life is, meet it and live it; do not <u>shun</u> it and call it hard names. It is not so bad as you are. It looks poorest when you are richest. The faultfinder will find faults even in paradise.</u> Love your life, poor as it is. You may perhaps have some pleasant, thrilling,

◆ Literary Analysis

Thoreau's **style** includes lots of figurative language, or language not meant to be taken literally. Circle an example of figurative language in the bracketed paragraph. What is the paragraph literally about? Circle the answer below.

(a) a person who cares about his or her status or position in society

(b) a nonconformist who does not go along with the crowd

(c) a soldier who bravely marches off to battle

(d) a musician who shows great talent and creativity

◆ Reading Strategy

Do you agree or disagree with the **writer's philosophy** expressed in the underlined passage? Explain your opinion.

_____

_____

_____

Vocabulary Development

haste (HAYST) *n.*　speed
enterprises (EN tuhr prī ziz) *n.*　projects; undertakings
pace (PAYS) *n.*　step
mean (MEEN) *adj.*　low; petty
shun (SHUN) *v.*　avoid

---

7. **measured:** slow and steady.

glorious hours, even in a poorhouse. <u>The setting sun is reflected from the windows of the almshouse[8] as brightly as from the rich man's abode;[9] the snow melts before its door as early in the spring.</u> I do not see but a quiet mind may live as <u>contentedly</u> there, and have as cheering thoughts, as in a palace. The town's poor seem to me often to live the most independent lives of any. Maybe they are simply great enough to receive without <u>misgiving</u>. Most think that they are above being supported by the town; but it oftener happens that they are not above supporting themselves by dishonest means, which should be more <u>disreputable</u>. <u>Cultivate poverty like a garden herb, like sage. Do not trouble yourself much to get new things, whether clothes or friends. Turn the old;[10] return to them. Things do not change; we change. Sell your clothes and keep your thoughts.</u>

◆ ◆ ◆

Thoreau concludes with a story about a local farm family. They have a sixty-year-old kitchen table made from the wood of an apple tree. One day the family hears odd sounds from deep inside the table. Then, after several weeks, out comes a strong, beautiful bug. It hatched from an egg that

Vocabulary Development

contentedly (kuhn TEN tid lee) *adv.* with happy satisfaction
misgiving (mis GIV ing) *n.* regret
disreputable (dis REP yuh tuh buhl) *adj.* having a bad reputation; considered bad by society
cultivate (KUL tuh vayt) *v.* grow; encourage

8. **almshouse** (AHMZ HOWS) *n.* a homeless shelter for the poor.
9. **abode** (uh BOHD) *n.* home; residence.
10. **Turn the old** turn worn old clothes inside out so that you can keep wearing them.

from Walden **101**

◆ **Stop to Reflect**

What does the underlined statement literally mean? Circle the letter of the best answer.

(a) Rich and poor alike can enjoy love and friendship in life.

(b) Rich and poor alike can enjoy the wonders of nature.

(c) It is better to be rich than poor.

(d) The people who deserve to be rich are rich, and the people who deserve to be poor are poor.

◆ **Reading Check**

What does Thoreau think is more important than clothes? Answer by circling a word in the underlined passage.

◆ **Reading Strategy**

Below, **evaluate the writer's philosophy** about the poor by circling whether you agree or disagree. Then, use your own knowledge or experiences to support your opinion.

(1) I agree/disagree that the poor are more independent.

(2) Support: _____

_____

_____

_____

_____

Mark the Text

had apparently been laid in the apple tree when it was still alive, sixty years before.

◆ ◆ ◆

Who knows what beautiful and winged life, whose egg has been buried for ages under many <u>concentric</u> layers of woodenness in the dead dry life of society, deposited at first in the alburnum[11] of the green and living tree, which has been gradually <u>converted</u> into the semblance of its well-seasoned tomb[12]—heard perchance[13] <u>gnawing</u> out now for years by the astonished family of man, as they sat round the festive board[14]—may unexpectedly come forth from amidst society's most trivial and handselled[15] furniture, to enjoy its perfect summer life at last!

I do not say that John or Jonathan[16] will realize all this; but such is the character of that morrow[17] which mere lapse of time can never make to dawn. The light which puts out our eyes is darkness to us. <u>Only that day dawns to which we are awake.</u> There is more day to dawn. The sun is but a morning star.

◆ **Literary Analysis**

Which elements of Thoreau's **style** are most clearly illustrated in the bracketed passage? Check two.

_____ simple language

_____ images from nature

_____ occasional short sentences

_____ figurative language

◆ **Stop to Reflect**

What does the underlined sentence mean?

_____

_____

_____

_____

_____

_____

Vocabulary Development

concentric (kuhn SEN trik) *adj.* with one circle inside another

converted (kuhn VER tid) *v.* changed

gnawing (NAW ing) *adj.* chewing

---

11. **alburnum** (al BUR nuhm) *n.* the soft wood between the bark and the core of the tree.
12. **the semblance** (SEM bluhns) **of its well-seasoned tomb** what seems like an aged tomb, or burial place.
13. **perchance** (puhr CHANS) *adv.* perhaps.
14. **festive** (FES tiv) **board** table.
15. **handselled** (HAN suhld) *adj.* handmade.
16. **John or Jonathan** average person.
17. **the morrow** (MAHR oh) the next day.

1. Complete these sentences about Thoreau by giving the main reasons for his actions.

   Thoreau went to live in the woods because _____.

   Thoreau left the woods because _____.

2. Thoreau's remark about the different drummer is now very famous. What do you think "to hear a different drummer" now means? Circle the letter of the best answer.

   (a) to give in to peer pressure   (c) to join the army or navy

   (b) not to go along with the crowd   (d) to compose classical music

3. Circle the attitudes or aspects of life that seem important to Thoreau.

   wealth   independence   competition   nature   simplicity   technology

4. **Literary Analysis:** On the chart below, list two examples of each element of Thoreau's **style**.

	Example 1	Example 2
Simple Language		
Images from Nature and Everyday Life		
Short Sentences		
Figurative Language		

5. **Reading Strategy:** Each sentence below expresses part of Thoreau's philosophy. Circle one sentence. Then, on the lines, **evaluate the philosophy** it expresses. Say whether Thoreau presents the idea clearly and supports it with enough examples and reasons. Compare the idea to your own knowledge and experience.

- Our life is frittered away by detail. . . Simplicity, simplicity, simplicity!
- However mean your life is, meet it and live it.
- Cultivate poverty like a garden herb, like sage.

_____

_____

Writing

Writing an Editorial

Would Thoreau's ideas about living simply work in today's world? Express your opinion in a one- or two-paragraph editorial.

- First, state your opinion about whether Thoreau's ideas on living simply would work today. State your opinion in a single sentence.

_____

_____

- Next, on separate paper, sum up Thoreau's ideas on living simply. Include at least one quotation from _Walden_ to support your summary.
- Finally, explain why you think Thoreau's ideas would or would not work in today's world. To support your opinion, include at least two reasons or examples from life today.
- Publish your editorial in the class or school newspaper.

An Episode of War
Stephen Crane

Summary

In this short story, a young Civil War
lieutenant is dividing his company's supply
of coffee when he is shot in the arm.
Treatment of the wounded is very poor,
but the lieutenant makes his way to the
field hospital. Before he gets to the hospital, another officer ties a handkerchief over
the wound. When the lieutenant sees a
doctor, the doctor assures him that he
will not amputate the arm. When the
lieutenant gets home, his mother, sisters,
and wife are sad that his arm has been
amputated.

Visual Summary

Setting:	**Place:** a battlefield during a lull in the fighting **Time:** the Civil War
Problem:	The lieutenant is wounded by a stray bullet.
	Event 1: The lieutenant is using his sword to divide coffee when he is unexpectedly shot in the arm.
	Event 2: Because of his wound, the lieutenant has trouble getting his sword back into the scabbard.
	Event 3: Another soldier helps him with the sword without touching him.
	Event 4: The lieutenant leaves to find a field hospital.
	Event 5: On his way to the field hospital, the lieutenant meets an officer who ties a handkerchief over the lieutenant's wound.
	Event 6: The lieutenant finds the field hospital, where conditions are terrible.
Climax:	**(Turning Point):**
	The lieutenant tells the doctor that he does not want his arm to be amputated.
Resolution:	**(Conclusion):**
	The lieutenant loses his arm in spite of the doctor's promise.

LITERARY ANALYSIS

Realism and Naturalism

Two literary movements became popular during the mid- to late-1800s: Realism and Naturalism. Both reacted against Romanticism, a style that emphasized emotion, imagination, and nature.

- **Realism** aimed to portray life faithfully and accurately. Realistic writers focused on ordinary people in everyday life.
- The goal of **Naturalism** was also to present ordinary people's lives. However, the Naturalist writers also suggested that people's fate was shaped by forces they could not control. Among these powerful forces were environment, heredity, and chance.

As you read "An Episode of War," look for elements related to these two literary movements.

READING STRATEGY

Recognizing Historical Details

Stories often reflect the time and place in which they were written. When you **recognize historical details**, you identify how the attitudes of the characters and the events of a story reflect the ideas of their time. "An Episode of War" takes place during the Civil War (1861-1865). You can therefore expect that many of the details in the story will reflect the conditions of life during that period.

As you read, use this chart to record details that are connected to the historical context.

Event	Historical Context
Battles	
Medical Practices	
Social Attitudes	

An Episode of War
Stephen Crane

The lieutenant's rubber blanket lay on the ground, and upon it he had poured the company's supply of coffee. Corporals and other representatives of the grimy and hot-throated men who lined the breast-work[1] had come for each squad's portion.

The lieutenant was frowning and serious at this task of division. His lips pursed as he drew with his sword various crevices in the heap, until brown squares of coffee, <u>astoundingly</u> equal in size, appeared on the blanket. He was on the verge of a great triumph in mathematics, and the corporals were thronging forward, each to reap a little square, when suddenly the lieutenant cried out and looked quickly at a man near him as if he suspected it was a case of personal assault. The others cried out also when they saw blood upon the lieutenant's sleeve.

◆ ◆ ◆

The lieutenant stares at the forest in the distance. He sees little puffs of smoke from the gunfire. The lieutenant holds his sword in his left hand. He struggles to put it in its scabbard, or holder. An orderly-sergeant helps him. The men stare thoughtfully at the wounded lieutenant.

◆ ◆ ◆

There were others who <u>proffered</u> assistance. One timidly presented his shoulder and asked the lieutenant if he cared to lean upon it, but the latter[2] waved him away mournfully.

Vocabulary Development

astoundingly (uh STOWN ding lee) *adv.* amazingly
proffered (PRAH ferd) *v.* offered

---

1. **breast-work** low wall put up quickly as a defense in battle.
2. **the latter** the second in a list of two people or things; here, "the latter" refers to the lieutenant.

◆ **Reading Strategy**

Circle two details in the first paragraph that reflect the **historical context** of the story.

◆ **Stop to Reflect**

What do you think has happened to the lieutenant?

_____

_____

_____

◆ **Reading Check**

How does one soldier offer to help the lieutenant?

_____

_____

_____

_____

◆ **Literary Analysis**

Circle the word in the underlined sentence that best expresses the **Naturalists'** view that human beings are shaped by forces that they cannot control.

◆ **Literary Analysis**

How is this passage an example of **Realistic** writing, or writing that tries to portray life accurately?

_____

_____

_____

_____

_____

◆ **Reading Check**

What building serves as the center of the army field hospital? Circle the correct word in this sentence.

He wore the look of one who knows he is the victim of a terrible disease and understands his helplessness. He again stared over the breast-work at the forest, and then, turning, went slowly rearward. He held his right wrist tenderly in his left hand as if the wounded arm was made of very <u>brittle</u> glass.

And the men in silence stared at the wood, then at the departing lieutenant: then at the wood, then at the lieutenant.

As the wounded officer passed from the line of battle, he was enabled to see many things which as a participant in the fight were unknown to him. He saw a general on a black horse gazing over the lines of blue infantry at the green woods which veiled his problems. An aide galloped furiously, dragged his horse suddenly to a halt, saluted, and presented a paper. It was, for a wonder, precisely like a historical painting.

◆　◆　◆

The lieutenant observes the swirling movement of a crew of men with heavy guns. The shooting crackles like brush-fires. The lieutenant comes across some stragglers. They tell him how to find the field hospital. At the roadside, an officer uses his handkerchief to bandage the lieutenant's wound.

◆　◆　◆

The low white tents of the hospital were grouped around an old schoolhouse. There was here a singular[3] commotion.

Vocabulary Development

brittle (BRIT tuhl) *adj.* stiff and easily broken

---

3. **singular** (SING yoo luhr) *adj.* remarkable, noticeable.

In the foreground two ambulances interlocked wheels in the deep mud. The drivers were tossing the blame of it back and forth, gesticulating[4] and berating,[5] while from the ambulances, both crammed with wounded, there came an occasional groan. An <u>interminable</u> crowd of bandaged men were coming and going. Great numbers sat under the trees nursing heads or arms or legs. There was a <u>dispute</u> of some kind raging on the steps of the schoolhouse. Sitting with his back against a tree a man with a face as grey as a new army blanket was <u>serenely</u> smoking a corncob pipe. The lieutenant wished to rush forward and inform him that he was dying.

◆ ◆ ◆

A doctor greets the lieutenant and notices his wounded arm. The doctor looks at the wound.

◆ ◆ ◆

The doctor cried out impatiently, "What mutton-head had tied it up that way anyhow?" The lieutenant answered, "Oh, a man."

When the wound was disclosed the doctor fingered it <u>disdainfully</u>. "Humph," he said. "You come along with me and I'll 'tend to you." His voice contained the same scorn as if he were saying: "You will have to go to jail."

◆ Read Fluently

Read the bracketed passage aloud. What impression does the passage give you of conditions at the field hospital?

_____

_____

_____

◆ Reading Check

Who bandages the lieutenant's arm?

_____

_____

_____

◆ Stop to Reflect

What does the doctor's attitude toward the lieutenant show about the doctor?

_____

_____

_____

Vocabulary Development

interminable (in TERM uh nuh buhl) *adj.* endless

dispute (dis PYOOT) *n.* disagreement

serenely (suh REEN lee) *adv.* calmly

disdainfully (dis DAYN fuh lee) *adv.* scornfully

---

4. **gesticulating** (jes TIK yoo layt ing) *v.* making vigorous gestures.
5. **berating** (bee RAYT ing) *v.* criticizing harshly.

© Pearson Education, Inc.

An Episode of War **109**

The lieutenant had been very <u>meek</u>, but now his face was flushed, and he looked into the doctor's eyes. "I guess I won't have it <u>amputated</u>," he said.

"Nonsense, man! Nonsense! Nonsense!" cried the doctor. "Come along, now. I won't amputate it. Come along. Don't be a baby."

"Let go of me," said the lieutenant, holding back <u>wrathfully</u>, his glance fixed upon the door of the old schoolhouse, as sinister to him as the portals[6] of death.

And this is the story of how the lieutenant lost his arm. When he reached home, his sisters, his mother, his wife, sobbed for a long time at the sight of the flat sleeve. "Oh, well," he said, standing shamefaced in the midst of these tears, "I don't suppose it matters so much as all that."

◆ **Reading Strategy**

How is the end of the story an example of **Naturalistic** writing, or writing that assumes that people are influenced by forces they cannot control?

_____

_____

_____

Vocabulary Development

meek (MEEK) *adj.* humble, mild-mannered
amputated (AMP yoo tay tuhd) *v.* cut off
wrathfully (RATH fuh lee) *adv.* angrily

---

6. **portals** (PORT uhlz) *n.* doors.

1. What happens to the lieutenant when he is dividing the portions of coffee?

   _____

   _____

2. Identify three people in the story who offer help to the lieutenant.

   (a) _____

   (b) _____

   (c) _____

3. When the lieutenant arrives at the schoolhouse, what has happened to cause a commotion?

   _____

   _____

4. **Reading Strategy:** What **historical details** of Civil War medical practices do you learn in this story? List at least two.

   _____

   _____

5. **Literary Analysis:** According to the **Naturalists,** human beings are weak and at the mercy of powerful forces. In what way might this statement apply to "An Episode of War"?

   _____

   _____

Writing

A Field Report on Hospital Conditions

Assume that a colonel in the Civil War wants to know why so many of his soldiers are dying from minor wounds. Imagine that you are the lieutenant in "An Episode of War." Write a report to the colonel on the medical treatment you received at the field hospital. In your report, describe the problems you observed at the hospital.

As you plan your report, consider the following conditions of Civil War medical care:

- Barns, warehouses, and schools often served as makeshift hospitals.
- Hospitals were understaffed and underequipped. There were few nurses.
- Medicines were in short supply.
- Amputation was the routine treatment for injured limbs.
- Twice as many soldiers died of infections as died of combat wounds.

In your report, support your main ideas with **precise details**. You can take some of these details from the story. For example, you might want to refer to the shouting match between the ambulance drivers, the endless crowds of bandaged men, or the doctor's promise that he would not amputate.

You can also use items drawn from the list of conditions shown above. Add specific details as appropriate. For example, you could describe the understaffing of hospitals vividly as follows:

We must have more medical staff immediately, or more men will die. The wounded are often neglected and forced to lie on filthy beds, or even on the floor, for hours and even days at a time. No one feeds, bathes, or treats them.

When you have finished a first draft of your report, check it for logical order and precise supporting details. Improve your organization if necessary. If you need to, add or rearrange details to strengthen or clarify your writing.

Share your report with your classmates.

from My Bondage and My Freedom

Frederick Douglass

Summary

While Frederick Douglass is a slave, his owner's wife begins to teach him to read. However, her husband convinces her that it is not a good idea to educate slaves, and Mrs. Auld becomes a different person. She keeps young Frederick from reading whenever she can. He continues to learn from white boys, paying them with bread. At the age of thirteen, he reads about liberty, and realizes that he and Mrs. Auld are both victims of slavery.

Visual Summary

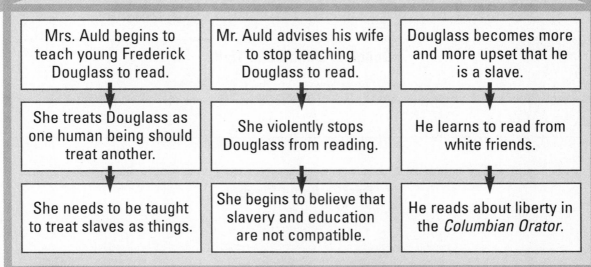

Main Idea

Both slaves and slave owners are victims of slavery.

Mrs. Auld begins to teach young Frederick Douglass to read.	Mr. Auld advises his wife to stop teaching Douglass to read.	Douglass becomes more and more upset that he is a slave.
She treats Douglass as one human being should treat another.	She violently stops Douglass from reading.	He learns to read from white friends.
She needs to be taught to treat slaves as things.	She begins to believe that slavery and education are not compatible.	He reads about liberty in the *Columbian Orator*.

LITERARY ANALYSIS

Autobiography

An **autobiography** is a person's written account of his or her own life. The author of an autobiography tells about the events that he or she considers most important.

In an autobiography, the writer's life is presented as he or she views it. Therefore, the portrayal of people and events is influenced by the author's feelings and beliefs.

Usually, writers of autobiographies believe that their lives can help others in some way. Frederick Douglass, for example, wrote his autobiography because he believed that his life could serve as an example to others.

As you read the experiences that shaped Douglass's life, notice how the events and feelings he describes might serve as examples for others.

READING STRATEGY

Establishing a Purpose

You can improve your understanding of what you read by **establishing a purpose** for your reading. As you read from Douglass's autobiography, for example, you might establish this two-part purpose:

- To learn about Douglass's special qualities of character.
- To expand your understanding of what it was like to be a slave.

Use this chart to record details reflecting your purpose.

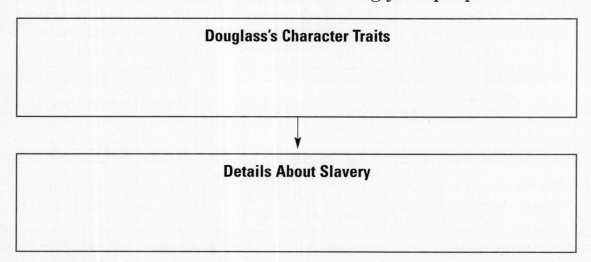

Douglass's Character Traits

Details About Slavery

from My Bondage and My Freedom
Frederick Douglass

I lived in the family of Master Hugh, at Baltimore, seven years, during which time— as the almanac makers say of the weather— my condition was variable. The most interesting feature of my history here, was my learning to read and write, under some- what marked disadvantages. In attaining this knowledge, I was compelled to resort to indirections by no means <u>congenial</u> to my nature, and which were really humiliating to me. My mistress—who had begun to teach me—was suddenly checked[1] in her <u>benevolent</u> design, by the strong advice of her husband. In faithful compliance with this advice, the good lady had not only ceased to instruct me, herself, but had set her face as a flint against my learning to read by any means.

◆   ◆   ◆

Douglass says that nature does not prepare people to be either slaves or slave- holders. At first, Mrs. Auld treats Douglass well. It takes a struggle inside her own soul to make her treat him as less than human.

◆   ◆   ◆

When I went into their family, it was the <u>abode</u> of happiness and contentment. The mistress of the house was a model of affection and tenderness. Her fervent <u>piety</u> and watchful

---

Vocabulary Development

congenial (kuhn JEEN yuhl) *adj.* agreeable
benevolent (buh NEV uh luhnt) *adj.* kindly, charitable
abode (uh BOHD) *n.* home
piety (PĪ uh tee) *n.* devotion to religious beliefs or practices

---

1. **checked** stopped, prevented.

uprightness made it impossible to see her without thinking and feeling—"that woman is a Christian." There was no sorrow nor suffering for which she had not a tear, and there was no innocent joy for which she did not [have] a smile. She had bread for the hungry, clothes for the naked, and comfort for every mourner that came within her reach. Slavery soon proved its ability to divest[2] her of these excellent qualities, and her home of its early happiness.

◆   ◆   ◆

Mrs. Auld stops teaching Douglass. Then she becomes even more opposed than her husband to his learning to read. She angrily snatches a book or a newspaper from his hand.

◆   ◆   ◆

Mrs. Auld was an apt[3] woman, and the advice of her husband, and her own experience, soon demonstrated, to her entire satisfaction, that education and slavery are <u>incompatible</u> with each other. When this conviction was thoroughly established, I was most narrowly watched in all my movements. If I remained in a separate room from the family for any considerable length of time, I was sure to be suspected of having a book, and was at once called upon to give an account of myself.

◆   ◆   ◆

However, these efforts come too late to stop Douglass from learning to read.

◆   ◆   ◆

Vocabulary Development

incompatible (in kuhm PAT uh buhl) *adj.* not able to exist together with

---

2. **divest** (duh VEST) *v.* strip, remove from.
3. **apt** (APT) *adj.* quick to learn.

Seized with a determination to learn to read, at any cost, I hit upon many expedients[4] to accomplish the desired end. The plea which I mainly adopted, and the one by which I was most successful, was that of using my young white playmates, with whom I met in the street, as teachers. I used to carry, almost constantly, a copy of Webster's spelling book in my pocket; and, when sent on errands, or when play time was allowed me, I would step, with my young friends, aside, and take a lesson in spelling. I generally paid my *tuition fee* to the boys, with bread, which I also carried in my pocket.

◆ ◆ ◆

Douglass feels grateful to the boys, but he does not want to identify his teachers by name. They might get into trouble for helping him.

◆ ◆ ◆

Although slavery was a delicate subject, and very cautiously talked about among grownup people in Maryland, I frequently talked about it—and that very freely—with the white boys. I would, sometimes, say to them, while seated on a curbstone or a cellar door, "I wish I could be free, as you will be when you get to be men." "You will be free, you know, as soon as you are twenty-one, and can go where you like, but I am a slave for life. Have I not as good a right to be free as you have?" Words like these, I observed, always troubled them; and I had no small satisfaction in wringing from the boys, occasionally, that fresh and bitter condemnation of slavery, that springs from nature, unseared and unperverted.[5]

◆ ◆ ◆

4. **expedients** (ek SPEE dee uhnts) *n.* ways of getting things done.
5. **unperverted** (un puhr VERT id) *adj.* uncorrupted, pure.

◆ **Read Fluently**

Read the bracketed passage aloud. How did Douglass accomplish his goal of learning to read?

_____

_____

_____

◆ **Reading Strategy**

One **purpose** for reading Douglass's account is to understand what it was like to be a slave. How does Douglass think his future will be different from the future of his white playmates?

_____

_____

_____

◆ **Reading Check**

How do human beings react by nature to slavery? Underline the phrase that gives Douglass's opinion.

Douglass never meets a boy who defends slavery. His love of liberty grows steadily. By age thirteen, he has learned to read. He buys a schoolbook. But the praise of liberty in what he reads makes him feel unhappy and depressed. He cannot bear the idea that he will be a slave all his life.

◆ ◆ ◆

Once awakened by the silver trump[6] of knowledge, my spirit was roused to eternal wakefulness. Liberty! the inestimable[7] birthright of every man, had, for me, converted every object into an asserter of this great right. It was heard in every sound, and beheld in every object. It was ever present, to torment me with a sense of my wretched condition. The more beautiful and charming were the smiles of nature, the more horrible and desolate was my condition. I saw nothing without seeing it, and I heard nothing without hearing it. I do not exaggerate, when I say, that it looked from every star, smiled in every calm, breathed in every wind, and moved in every storm.

◆ ◆ ◆

Douglass has no doubt that Mrs. Auld notices his attitude. While nature has made them friends, slavery has made them enemies. Douglass is not cruelly treated, but he still hates the condition of slavery.

◆ ◆ ◆

I had been cheated. I saw through the attempt to keep me in ignorance . . . The feeding and clothing me well, could not <u>atone</u> for taking my liberty from me. The smiles of my mistress could not remove the deep sorrow

Vocabulary Development

atone (uh TOHN) *v.* make up for

6. **trump** trumpet.
7. **inestimable** (in ES tuh muh buhl) *adj.* priceless.

◆ Reading Strategy

One **purpose for reading** Douglass's account is to understand his character. From the evidence of the bracketed passage, how does Douglass feel about being a slave?

_____

_____

_____

◆ Stop to Reflect

Why does Douglass say that he has been cheated?

_____

_____

_____

_____

that dwelt in my young bosom. Indeed, these, in time, came only to deepen my sorrow. She had changed; and the reader will see that I had changed, too. We were both victims of the same overshadowing evil—*she,* as mistress, *I,* as slave. I will not <u>censure</u> her harshly; she cannot censure me, for she knows I speak but the truth, and have acted in my opposition to slavery, just as she herself would have acted, in a reverse of circumstances.

◆　◆　◆

◆ **Stop to Reflect**

How was Douglass's mistress a "victim," in your opinion?

_____

_____

_____

Vocabulary Development

censure (SEN shuhr) *v.* condemn as wrong

---

from My Bondage and My Freedom **119**

1. Why does Mrs. Auld stop teaching Douglass how to read?

_____

_____

2. How does Douglass finally learn to read?

_____

_____

3. What attitude do the white boys have about slavery?

_____

_____

4. What event transforms Douglass, making him feel unhappy and depressed?

_____

_____

5. **Reading Strategy:** By **establishing a purpose** for reading, you can focus on an idea or concept in a passage. Use this chart to identify what you learned about the effects of slavery from Douglass's account.

Douglass's Account	**Effects of Slavery**
_____ →	_____
_____	_____
_____	_____

6. **Literary Analysis:** In an **autobiography,** the author presents people and events from his or her personal point of view. In what ways would this account be different if it had been written by Mrs. Auld?

_____

_____

Listening and Speaking

An Oral Presentation

Frederick Douglass was a gifted public speaker, as well as a powerful writer. Assume that you are making a speech to an audience of abolitionists, or those opposed to slavery. In your speech, you will use parts of Douglass's autobiography, together with statements of your own for emphasis.

Choose passages from the selection that you think are especially strong in opposing slavery. Here is a list of passages you might consider:

- THE PASSAGE BEGINNING "When I went into their family, it was the abode of happiness and contentment . . ." AND ENDING " . . . and her home of its early happiness." (pages 115–116)
- THE PASSAGE BEGINNING "Although slavery was a delicate subject . . ." AND ENDING " . . . that springs from nature, unseared and unperverted." (page 117)
- THE PASSAGE BEGINNING "Once awakened by the silver trump of knowledge . . ." AND ENDING " . . . breathed in every wind, and moved in every storm." (page 118)

Add statements of your own for emphasis. Make your statements consistent with Douglass's intent and purpose. Here are some guidelines for preparing your speech:

- When you are reading Douglass's exact words, make sure you identify the passage as a quotation from him.
- Use punctuation marks to guide your reading. Pause slightly for a comma. Make a full stop at a period.
- Note where Douglass uses parallel structure and repetition. Bring out these devices in your reading.
- Add strong emotion to convey Douglass's tone.
- When you use your own words, choose persuasive language to compel your audience.

After you have rehearsed your oral presentation, deliver it to the class.

The Notorious Jumping Frog of Calaveras County

Mark Twain

Summary

In this short story, the narrator asks a talkative old man, Simon Wheeler, about a man named Leonidas W. Smiley. Instead of talking about Leonidas W. Smiley, Wheeler tells a tall tale about a man named Jim Smiley. Jim loves to gamble and will bet on anything. He bets a stranger that his frog can outjump any frog in Calaveras County. The stranger accepts the bet, but he needs a frog. Jim goes to find one, and the stranger fills Jim's frog with lead pellets. The pellets make the frog too heavy to jump, so the stranger wins the bet. Jim discovers the trick, but he can't catch up with the stranger. Wheeler has more to tell, but the narrator leaves.

Visual Summary

Simon Wheeler's Story						
1. ⟶	**2.** ⟶	**3.** ⟶	**4.** ⟶	**5.** ⟶	**6.** ⟶	**7.**
Smiley will bet on a horse race, a cat or dog fight, a chicken fight—anything.	Once Smiley bet on the life of Parson Walker's wife.	Smiley owned a horse who won races at the last minute and a dog who won fights by grabbing the other dog's leg—until he was up against a dog with no hind legs.	Once Smiley had a frog—he named him Daniel Webster and taught him to jump.	A stranger offers to bet against Daniel Webster, but he has no frog. Smiley goes to find the stranger a frog.	While Smiley is gone, the stranger fills Smiley's frog's mouth with quailshot.	Smiley's frog loses. By the time Smiley discovers the quailshot, the stranger is long gone.

LITERARY ANALYSIS

Humor

Humor is writing intended to make you laugh. Humorists use many techniques to make their work funny. Many western humorists of the 1800s, like Mark Twain, use these techniques:

- They exaggerate or overstate events out of all proportion to their importance.
- They add many imaginative or ridiculous details.
- They use a narrator or a storyteller who speaks in a serious tone.
- They suggest that the teller of the story doesn't realize that the story is ridiculous.

As you read Mark Twain's story about a jumping frog, take note of the details that make the tale a classic of humor.

READING STRATEGY

Understanding Regional Dialect

Twain uses language colorfully, often with humorous results. He was a master at including regional dialect in his stories. **Regional dialect** is language specific to a particular area of the country.

At first sight, some of the words and phrases in dialect may seem like words you have never seen or heard before. If you read those unfamiliar words aloud, however, you will usually find that they are regional pronunciations of words you already know.

Use a chart like this one to translate dialect into modern Standard English.

Regional Dialect
. . . he was the curiousest man about always betting on anything that turned up you ever see, if he could get anybody to bet on the other side.

↓

Standard English
He was determined to bet on anything he could, if he could get someone to bet on the other side.

The Notorious Jumping Frog of Calaveras County **123**

The Notorious Jumping Frog of Calaveras County

Mark Twain

A friend of the narrator's asks him to call on talkative old Simon Wheeler. The friend says he wants news of his friend Reverend Leonidas W. Smiley. Instead, Wheeler tells the narrator a long-drawn-out story about Jim Smiley. As he tells the story, Wheeler never smiles, and he never frowns.

◆ ◆ ◆

"Rev. Leonidas W. H'm, Reverend Le—well, there was a feller here once by the name of Jim Smiley, in the winter of '49—or maybe it was the spring of '50—I don't <u>recollect</u> exactly, somehow, though what makes me think it was one or the other is because I remember the big flume[1] warn't finished when he first come to the camp; but anyway, he was the curiousest man about always betting on anything that turned up you ever see, if he could get anybody to bet on the other side; and if he couldn't he'd change sides.

◆ ◆ ◆

Wheeler says Smiley was lucky. He almost always won his bets. He'd bet on horse races, dog fights, cat fights, and chicken fights. If he saw two birds sitting on a fence, he'd bet on which bird would fly first. He had several animals he'd bet on: a mare, a small bull-pup named Andrew Jackson, and lots of others. One day he caught a frog, taught him to catch flies, and named him Dan'l Webster.

◆ ◆ ◆

Vocabulary Development

recollect (rek uh LEKT) *v.* remember

---

1. **flume** (FLOOM) *n.* artificial channel for carrying water to provide power and transport objects.

Well, Smiley kep' the beast in a little lattice box, and he used to fetch him downtown some- times and lay for a bet. One day a feller—a stranger in the camp, he was—come acrost him with his box, and says:

"What might it be that you've got in the box?"

And Smiley says, sorter indifferent-like, "It might be a parrot, or it might be a canary, maybe, but it ain't—it's only just a frog."

And the feller took it, and looked at it careful, and turned it round this way and that, and says, "H'm—so 'tis. Well, what's *he* good for?"

"Well," Smiley says, easy and careless, "he's good enough for *one* thing, I should judge—he can outjump any frog in Calaveras county."

The feller took the box again, and took another long, particular look, and gave it back to Smiley, and says, very underline{deliberate}, "Well," he says, "I don't see no p'ints[2] about that frog that's any better'n any other frog."

"Maybe you don't," Smiley says. "Maybe you understand frogs and maybe you don't under- stand 'em; maybe you've had experience, and maybe you ain't only a amature,[3] as it were. Anyways, I've got *my* opinion, and I'll resk forty dollars that he can outjump any frog in Calaveras county."

And the feller studied a minute, and then says, kinder sad like, "Well, I'm only a stranger here, and I ain't got no frog; but if I had a frog, I'd bet you."

◆   ◆   ◆

Vocabulary Development

deliberate (di LIB rit) *adj.* carefully thought out

2. **p'ints** dialect for *points,* meaning fine points or advantages.
3. **amature** dialect for *amateur* (AM uh chuhr) *n.* unskillful person.

◆ **Reading Strategy**

Rewrite the underlined passage of **regional dialect** in standard English.

_____
_____
_____

◆ **Stop to Reflect**

Why do you suppose Smiley seems "indifferent" and indirect in his answer to the stranger?

_____
_____
_____

◆ **Read Fluently**

Read the bracketed paragraph aloud. What does this description of the stranger suggest about his personality?

_____
_____
_____

◆ **Literary Analysis**

Smiley's long-drawn-out answer adds to the **humor**. Underline the word he repeats several times in order to spin out his answer to the stranger.

Mark the Text

◆ Reading Strategy

Circle two words in the bracketed passage that are examples of **regional dialect**.

◆ Literary Analysis

How do these details about what the stranger does to Smiley's frog add to the story's **humor**?

_____

_____

_____

◆ ◆ ◆

So he set there a good while thinking and thinking to hisself, and then he got the frog out and prized his mouth open and took a tea-spoon and filled him full of quailshot[4]—filled him pretty near up to his chin—and set him on the floor. Smiley he went to the swamp and slopped around in the mud for a long time, and finally he ketched a frog, and fetched him in, and give him to this feller, and says:

"Now, if you're ready, set him alongside of Dan'l, with his forepaws just even with Dan'l's, and I'll give the word." Then he says, "One—two—three—*git!*" and him and the feller touched up the frogs from behind, and the new frog hopped off lively, but Dan'l give a heave, and hysted[5] up his shoulders—so—like a Frenchman, but it warn't no use—he couldn't budge; he was planted as solid as a church, and he couldn't no more stir than if he was anchored out. Smiley was a good deal surprised, and he was disgusted too, but he didn't have no idea what the matter was, of course.

The feller took the money and started away, and when he was going out at the door, he sorter jerked his thumb over his shoulder—so—at Dan'l, and says again, very deliberate, "Well," he says, "I don't see no p'ints about that frog that's any better'n any other frog."

Smiley he stood scratching his head and looking down at Dan'l a long time, and at last he says, "I do wonder what in the nation that frog throw'd off for—I wonder if there ain't something the matter with him—he 'pears to

---

4. **quailshot** small lead pellets used for shooting quail.
5. **hysted** dialect for *hoisted*, meaning raised.

look mighty baggy, somehow." And he ketched Dan'l by the nap of the neck, and hefted him, and says, "Why blame my cats if he don't weigh five pound!" and turned him upside down and he belched out a double handful of shot. And then he see how it was, and he was the maddest man—he set the frog down and took out after that feller, but he never ketched him. And—

◆   ◆   ◆

At this point someone calls Wheeler from the front yard. The narrator knows that Wheeler has no information about the Rev. Leonidas W. Smiley, so he starts to leave. He meets Wheeler at the door, and Wheeler says:

◆   ◆   ◆

"Well, thish-yer Smiley had a yaller one-eyed cow that didn't have no tail, only just a short stump like a bannanner, and—"

However, lacking both time and <u>inclination</u>, I did not wait to hear about the afflicted cow, but took my leave.

◆ **Reading Check**

When Smiley found out how he had been tricked, what was his reaction?

_____

_____

_____

◆ **Literary Analysis**

What do you think Wheeler is about to do now? How does that contribute to the **humor** of the story?

_____

_____

_____

Vocabulary Development

inclination (in kluh NAY shuhn) *n.* liking or preference

---

1. What was Jim Smiley's response to any event?

_____

_____

2. Why was Smiley so proud of his frog?

_____

_____

3. What caused Smiley to lose his bet to the stranger?

_____

_____

4. How does this story reveal the character of Simon Wheeler as well as it shows the character of Jim Smiley? Explain your answer.

_____

_____

5. **Literary Analysis:** One technique Twain uses to create **humor** is exaggeration, or overstatement. On the chart below, identify two examples of exaggeration. Then explain why each is amusing.

Exaggeration	
Example 1: _____	Example 2: _____
_____	_____
Why It Is Amusing: _____	Why It Is Amusing: _____
_____	_____

6. **Reading Strategy:** The language specific to a particular area of the country is called **regional dialect**. Rewrite the following passage in your own words:

"Well, thish-yer Smiley had a yaller one-eyed cow that didn't have no tail, only just a short stump like a bannanner . . ."

_____

_____

Writing

Analytic Essay

Mark Twain once described the techniques a writer uses to create humor this way:

"The humorous story may be spun out to great length, and may wander around as much as it pleases, and arrive at nowhere in particular . . . [It] is told gravely; the teller does his best to conceal the fact that he even dimly suspects there is anything funny about it."

Write an essay discussing Twain's use of these humorous techniques in "The Notorious Jumping Frog of Calaveras County."

1. Start by choosing passages from the story that serve as examples of Twain's main ideas as quoted in the passage above. Use this chart to organize your thoughts:

Idea	spins out at length	arrives nowhere	is told gravely	conceals humor
Example				

2. As you continue work on your essay, keep these guidelines in mind.
   - Organize your paper point by point, connecting each of Twain's ideas to passages from the story.
   - Make sure you clearly explain the connection in each case.

3. Review your first draft to find places you could improve. For example, you might add examples, details, or quotations to support your ideas.

4. Share your essay with a small group of classmates. Use their suggestions to make additional revisions.

The Story of an Hour
Kate Chopin

Summary

When Mrs. Mallard hears that her husband has been killed in a train accident, she cries and goes to her room. Alone there, she realizes that she is free from the control of her husband. As she leaves her room, she is very happy. Just then, her husband, who had not been on the train after all, comes in the door. Mrs. Mallard dies of a heart attack.

Visual Summary

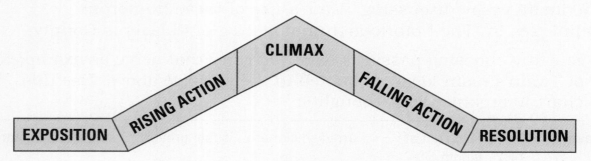

EXPOSITION	RISING ACTION	CLIMAX	FALLING ACTION	RESOLUTION
Mrs. Mallard has a weak heart. Her sister and Richards, a close family friend, tell her carefully of the death of her husband in a train accident.	Mrs. Mallard weeps immediately. Then she goes to her room and gradually begins to feel the freedom of being able to live for herself.	Mrs. Mallard leaves her room in a sort of triumph. As she goes downstairs, she sees her husband coming in the door.	Mrs. Mallard's sister cries out, Richards tries to shield Mrs. Mallard from the sight of her husband, and Mr. Mallard is amazed.	Mrs. Mallard dies of a heart attack. The doctors say it was caused by joy, but the reader knows the real cause.

LITERARY ANALYSIS

Irony

Irony is a literary technique involving a contradiction or a sharp difference. Sometimes, an irony exists between what a speaker says and what he or she really means. Other times, irony may result from a difference between what is expected and what actually happens. Irony can be surprising, interesting, or amusing.

When you read literature, you will frequently meet three types of irony:

Type of Irony	Nature of Contrast
Verbal irony	Words suggest the opposite of their usual meaning.
Dramatic irony	Readers are aware of something that a character does not know.
Situational irony	The outcome of an action or situation is very different from what we expect.

As you read "The Story of an Hour," decide which type of irony best fits the story.

READING STRATEGY

Recognizing Ironic Details

When you read a story, the details in it often lead you to expect certain events. When events do not turn out the way you expect, you experience a sense of irony. Looking back, you can **recognize ironic details**.

While you read "The Story of an Hour," use this chart to note ironic details. On the chart, write events or feelings that do not turn out to be what they appear to be at first.

Detail →	Expected outcome →	Actual outcome
Care is taken to reveal bad news to Mrs. Mallard.	She would be upset.	

The Story of an Hour
Kate Chopin

Knowing that Mrs. Mallard was afflicted[1] with a heart trouble, great care was taken to break to her as gently as possible the news of her husband's death.

It was her sister Josephine who told her, in broken sentences; veiled hints that revealed in half concealing. Her husband's friend Richards was there too, near her. It was he who had been in the newspaper office when intelligence[2] of the railroad disaster was received, with Brently Mallard's name leading the list of "killed." He had only taken the time to assure himself of its truth by a second telegram, and had hastened to <u>forestall</u> any less careful, less tender friend in bearing the sad message.

◆ ◆ ◆

Mrs. Mallard bursts out weeping in her sister's arms. She goes to her room alone. There she sits in a chair facing the open window.

◆ ◆ ◆

She could see in the open square before her house the tops of trees that were all aquiver with the new spring life. The delicious breath of rain was in the air. In the street below a peddler was crying his wares.[3] The notes of a distant song which someone was singing reached her faintly, and countless sparrows were twittering in the eaves.

Vocabulary Development

forestall (fawr STAWL) *v.* prevent by acting ahead of time

1. **afflicted** (uh FLIK ted) *adj.* suffering from.
2. **intelligence** (in TEL i juhnts) *n.* news.
3. **wares** (wayrz) *n.* merchandise.

◆ **Stop to Reflect**

Why is Richards careful to be sure that the message is true?

_____

_____

_____

◆ **Reading Strategy**

Mrs. Mallard has just received news of her husband's death. Circle three **details** in the bracketed passage that you recognize as **ironic** under the circumstances.

There were patches of blue sky showing here and there through the clouds that had met and piled one above the other in the west facing her window.

◆ ◆ ◆

Mrs. Mallard still sobs occasionally. She stares dully at the sky. Then she senses a new emotion coming over her. She tries to fight her new feelings, but her effort is not successful.

◆ ◆ ◆

When she abandoned herself,[4] a little whispered word escaped her slightly parted lips. She said it over and over under her breath: "free, free, free!" The vacant stare and the look of terror that had followed it went from her eyes. They stayed keen and bright. Her pulses beat fast, and the coursing blood warmed and relaxed every inch of her body.

She did not stop to ask if it were or were not a monstrous joy that held her. A clear and exalted perception enabled her to dismiss the suggestion as trivial.

She knew that she would weep again when she saw the kind, tender hands folded in death; the face that had never looked save with love upon her, fixed and gray and dead. But she saw beyond that bitter moment a long procession of years to come that would belong to her absolutely. And she opened and spread her arms out to them in welcome.

There would be no one to live for her during

◆ Read Fluently

Read the underlined paragraph aloud. What might the "patches of blue sky" showing through the clouds suggest about a change in Mrs. Mallard's mood?

_____

_____

_____

◆ Literary Analysis

What **irony**, or contrast, does this bracketed passage reveal between what was expected and what actually happens?

_____

_____

_____

◆ Reading Strategy

Remember that an **ironic detail** may not turn out to be what it seems. What does the phrase "a long procession of years" lead you to expect?

_____

_____

_____

Vocabulary Development

trivial (TRIV i uhl) *adj.* unimportant

---

4. **abandoned herself** surrendered or gave herself up.

What attitude toward marriage is expressed in the underlined sentence?

_____

_____

_____

_____

those coming years; she would live for herself. There would be no powerful will bending hers in that blind persistence with which men and women believe they have a right to impose a private will upon a fellow creature.

◆   ◆   ◆

Mrs. Mallard reflects on her new-found freedom. Compared to the future, the past matters little. Suddenly she hears her sister Josephine begging her to open the door. Mrs. Mallard dreams of her future life a little longer. She prays for a long life. Then she opens the door and puts her arm around her sister. They go down the stairs together. At the bottom, Richards stands waiting for them.

◆   ◆   ◆

Someone was opening the front door with a latchkey. It was Brently Mallard who entered, a little travel-stained, composedly[5] carrying his gripsack[6] and umbrella. He had been far from the scene of the accident, and did not know there had been one. He stood amazed at Josephine's piercing cry; at Richards's quick motion to screen him from the view of his wife.

But Richards was too late.

When the doctors came they said she had died of heart disease—of joy that kills.

◆ Reading Check

How is it possible for Brently Mallard to be alive and well?

_____

_____

_____

◆ Literary Analysis

In **verbal irony**, words suggest the opposite of their usual meaning. Underline the phrase in this sentence that is an example of verbal irony.

5. **composedly** (kum POHZ uhd le) *adj.* calmly.
6. **gripsack** (GRIP sak) *n.* small bag for holding clothes.

1. At the beginning of the story, the narrator says that Mrs. Mallard suffers from a "heart trouble." What, in addition to a medical condition, might the narrator mean by this phrase?

_____

_____

2. On the chart below, list four details that Mrs. Mallard sees, hears, or senses outside her window.

Detail 1	Detail 3
Detail 2	Detail 4

3. In what way do these sights, smells, and sounds outside foreshadow, or predict, the feelings that sweep over Mrs. Mallard?

_____

_____

4. Mrs. Mallard repeatedly whispers the word "free" to herself. What has she apparently resented about her marriage?

_____

_____

5. **Literary Analysis:** When events turn out contrary to what we expect, the result is **situational irony**. In what ways are Brently Mallard's return and Mrs. Mallard's death examples of situational irony?

_____

_____

6. **Reading Strategy:** When you **recognize ironic details**, you realize that the actual outcome of an event or situation is very different from the expected outcome. What detail in the story's second paragraph makes Mr. Mallard's arrival at the end all the more ironic?

_____

_____

Listening and Speaking

A Soliloquy

A **soliloquy** is a long speech made by a character who is alone. The character reveals private feelings to the reader or the audience.

Imagine that Brently Mallard had never returned. Present a soliloquy in which Mrs. Mallard reflects on her life ten years later. Consider the following questions:

- Has Mrs. Mallard's heart trouble improved, or not?

_____

- Where is she living now?

_____

- Has she remarried? If so, what is her new husband like? If Mrs. Mallard has not remarried, why not?

_____

_____

- Has she traveled? If so, what memorable sights has she seen?

_____

_____

As you plan your soliloquy, keep in mind these guidelines:
- Use the thoughts and feelings in the story to create a real voice for Mrs. Mallard. For example, from the story you know that Mrs. Mallard values freedom and independence. She also notices details, like the sights and sounds outside her window.
- A soliloquy shares inner thoughts and feelings.

Present your soliloquy to your classmates.

The Turtle *from* The Grapes of Wrath

John Steinbeck

Summary

Near a highway is a mass of tangled, dry grass full of seeds of every kind. The seeds are waiting for a way to travel. It might be the hem of a woman's skirt or the paw of a passing animal. A land turtle crawls over the grass toward the highway. A head of wild oats attaches itself to the turtle's front legs. With  great effort, the turtle gets onto the highway. A car driven by a woman swerves to avoid the turtle. A light truck driven by a man swerves and hits the turtle's shell. The turtle rolls off the highway on its shell. After a long time, the turtle rolls itself over. The head of oats falls off and the seeds spill out. As the turtle pulls itself along, its shell drags dirt over the seeds.

Visual Summary

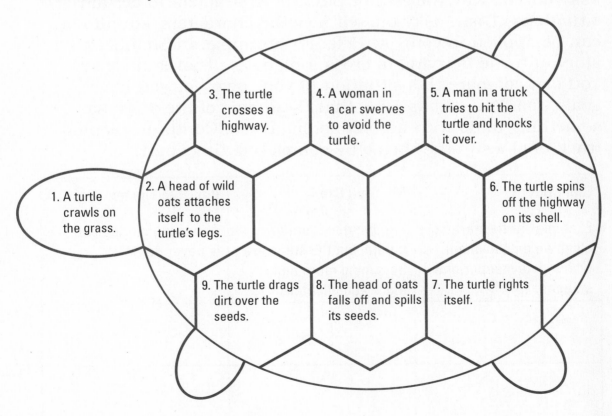

1. A turtle crawls on the grass.

2. A head of wild oats attaches itself to the turtle's legs.

3. The turtle crosses a highway.

4. A woman in a car swerves to avoid the turtle.

5. A man in a truck tries to hit the turtle and knocks it over.

6. The turtle spins off the highway on its shell.

7. The turtle rights itself.

8. The head of oats falls off and spills its seeds.

9. The turtle drags dirt over the seeds.

LITERARY ANALYSIS

Theme

A story's **theme** is its message about life. Authors reveal themes in these ways:

- Through what the characters say and do
- By what happens in the plot
- By using symbols, or details that stand for something else

In "The Turtle," John Steinbeck uses a turtle as a symbol for people. To figure out the theme of the story, consider these questions:

1. What is the turtle's goal?
2. What obstacles does the turtle face?
3. How does the turtle overcome the obstacles?

READING STRATEGY

Finding Clues to the Theme

When you read, look for **clues to the theme.** For example, ask yourself why the author puts the characters in certain situations. Then, ask yourself how the characters' situations can be applied to your own life. For example, in Steinbeck's story, a turtle is trying to cross a highway. That is his goal. You can compare this situation to your own, for you have goals, too. You can assume that the theme of the story has something to do with accomplishing goals. Continue keeping track of clues to the theme by completing this chart.

Story Detail	My Own Life	Possible Theme
Example: Turtle starts to climb an embankment, which gets steeper and steeper.	I'm trying to learn to dance, but the steps are becoming more and more complicated.	Achieving worthy goals is never easy.

The Turtle

John Steinbeck

Steinbeck opens by describing the land at the edge of a concrete highway. It is covered with a mat of dry grass full of various kinds of seeds. The seeds are waiting to be picked up by passing animals or to be carried by the wind.

Steinbeck continues by saying that the sun warms the grass. In the shade of the grass, many insects live.

◆　◆　◆

And over the grass at the roadside a land turtle crawled, <u>turning aside for nothing, dragging his high-domed shell over the grass</u>. His hard legs and yellow-nailed feet <u>threshed slowly through the grass, not really walking, but boosting and dragging his shell along</u>.

◆　◆　◆

The turtle does not notice seeds and burrs in his way. He moves ahead with his beak slightly open. His eyes stare straight ahead.

Steinbeck describes how the turtle moves across the grass. He leaves a trail behind him. The turtle sees a hill, which is really the highway <u>embankment</u>, ahead of him. Climbing the hill is a very difficult job for the turtle. Very slowly, he manages to get up the embankment. But then he gets to the shoulder of the highway. He faces what looks like a concrete wall. It is the concrete of the highway, four inches thick.

◆　◆　◆

◆ **Literary Analysis**

Read the underlined sections on this page. Then complete this sentence based on the **theme** of the story.

We can tell that the turtle is determined to get across the road because he does the following things:

he _____ ,

_____

and he _____

_____ .

Vocabulary Development

threshed (THRESHT) *v.*　struck over and over again

embankment (em BANGK ment) *n.*　a long mound of earth or stone that keeps water back or supports a road

◆ Reading Check

How does the turtle defend himself against the red ant?

_____

_____

_____

◆ Reading Strategy

To **find clues to the theme,** underline the part that tells how the woman acted when she saw the turtle. Circle the part on the next page that tells how the man in the truck acted. Then answer these questions:

(1) What do you think the woman symbolizes?

_____

(2) What do you think the man symbolizes?

_____

As though they worked independently the <u>hind</u> legs pushed the shell against the wall. The head upraised and peered over the wall to the broad smooth plain of cement.

◆ ◆ ◆

After much straining, the turtle lifts itself on the edge of the wall. As the turtle rests, a red ant runs into the turtle's shell. The turtle crushes it between its body and legs.

Steinbeck describes how some wild oat seeds are brought into the shell by the turtle's front leg. The turtle lies still for a moment. Then his head, legs, and tail come out of the shell. The turtle begins straining to reach the top of the cement. The hind legs slowly boost the rest of the turtle's body up. At last he gets to the top. The wild oat seeds are still attached around the turtle's front legs.

Movement is easy for the turtle now. The turtle begins to cross the highway.

◆ ◆ ◆

A <u>sedan</u> driven by a forty-year-old woman approached. She saw the turtle and swung to the right, off the highway, the wheels screamed and a cloud of dust boiled up.

◆ ◆ ◆

The car tips with the sudden swerve. After regaining control, the woman drives on slowly. The turtle had hidden in its shell in fear. But now the turtle hurries across the road.

◆ ◆ ◆

Vocabulary Development

hind (HĪND) *adj.* back
sedan (si DAN) *n.* a hard-top car big enough for four to seven people

And now a light truck approached, and as it came near, the driver saw the turtle and <u>swerved</u> to hit it.

◆ ◆ ◆

The front wheel of the truck hits the turtle. The turtle flips over and rolls off the highway.

Steinbeck describes how the turtle lies on its back. Its body is drawn into its shell. Finally, the legs come out and start waving around in the air. The turtle is looking for something to grab onto. At last its front foot gets hold of a piece of quartz. Very slowly, the turtle manages to pull itself over. At this point, the wild oat seeds fall out and get stuck in the ground.

As the turtle moves along, its shell buries the seeds with dirt.

◆ ◆ ◆

The turtle entered a dust road and jerked itself along, drawing a wavy shallow <u>trench</u> with its shell. The old humorous eyes looked ahead, and the horny beak opened a little. His yellow toe nails slipped a fraction in the dust.

◆ **Reading Check**

What position is the turtle in after the truck hits it?

_____

_____

_____

◆ **Stop to Reflect**

(1) How does the turtle help the wild oat seeds?

_____

_____

(2) What do you think Steinbeck is saying about how different forms of life relate to one another?

_____

_____

_____

Vocabulary Development

swerved (SWERVD) *v.* turned aside from a straight course
trench (TRENCH) *n.* a deep ditch dug in the ground

1. The dry, tangled grass by the highway is full of signs of life. Name three things that show this.

   1. _____ 2. _____ 3. _____

2. The turtle wants to cross the highway. But he runs into three problems that make it difficult for him to do so. Complete this chart by writing the three problems and then telling how the turtle deals with them.

Problems	How the Turtle Deals with Them

3. What does the turtle do to help the oat seeds?

   _____

   _____

4. The man in the light truck tries to hurt the turtle. How does his action actually help the turtle instead?

   _____

   _____

5. **Literary Analysis:** In the end, the turtle's shell drags dirt over the oat seeds. What **theme** is Steinbeck expressing here?

   _____

   _____

6. **Reading Strategy:** Put a check in front of the three details that you think are the best **clues to the theme.**

____ The turtle turned aside for nothing.

____ The turtle stared straight ahead.

____ The sedan was driven by a woman.

____ The light truck's driver was a man.

____ The turtle grabs onto a piece of quartz and pulls itself over.

Listening and Speaking

Conduct an Interview

Interview someone who lived during the Great Depression of the 1930s.

1. Choose the person you will interview.

_____

_____

2. Write three questions to ask during the interview.

1. _____

_____

2. _____

_____

3. _____

_____

3. Schedule your interview.

4. Ask your questions. You may follow either one of these methods:
   • Ask the person for permission to tape-record the interview, and then do so.
   • Take notes as the person answers your questions.

5. After you conduct the interview, get together with a small group and share the information you received.

The Far and the Near

Thomas Wolfe

Summary

For twenty years, the engineer of a train blows the whistle every day as he approaches a certain pleasant little cottage near the tracks. A woman and her daughter, both otherwise strangers to him, come out and wave to him as he passes. The women and the little house become symbols of happiness for him. At last, when he retires, he goes to visit the spot, to be near what he has only seen from the train for so long. At close range, though, the town is strange to him, the house is unattractive, and the women are unfriendly. He leaves, feeling disappointed, old, and sad.

Visual Summary

Sequence of Events					
1.	**2.**	**3.**	**4.**	**5.**	**6.**
For twenty years, a train engineer blows his whistle at a white cottage with green blinds.	A woman always comes out to wave. The engineer watches as her daughter grows up.	The women and the house become symbols of beauty and endurance for the engineer.	When the engineer retires, he decides to visit the women.	The town is different and the women are neither attractive nor friendly.	The engineer leaves, feeling old and discouraged.

LITERARY ANALYSIS
Climax and Anticlimax

A **climax** is the high point of a story. Sometimes that point is a letdown. It might be a disappointment to the characters. It might even be a disappointment to the reader. When this happens, it is called an **anticlimax.**

In "The Far and the Near," Thomas Wolfe tells the story of a train conductor. For twenty years, he drives through various towns across the United States. He sees these towns "from the high windows of his cab." In other words, he sees them from afar, like an outsider. One place in particular seems very attractive to him.

What do you think might happen when he has the chance to visit that place? Will it look the same when it becomes "the near" rather than "the far"?

READING STRATEGY
Predicting

When you **predict,** you tell what you think will happen next. Your prediction should be based on your knowledge of real life. Use your own experience and knowledge to help you make predictions.

As you read, practice making predictions by filling in this chart.

Story Detail	My Experience or Knowledge About This Detail	My Prediction
Example: Every day for more than twenty years	Many changes take place in twenty years.	The characters in the story will change.

The Far and the Near
Thomas Wolfe

The story opens with a description of a tidy little cottage. It is white with green blinds. It has a vegetable garden, a grape arbor, and flower beds. In front of the house are three big oak trees. The house looks neat and comfortable. Every afternoon, just after two o'clock, an express train passes by the house.

◆ ◆ ◆

Every day for more than twenty years, as the train had approached this house, the engineer had blown on the whistle, and every day, as soon as she heard this signal, a woman had appeared on the back porch of the little house and waved to him.

◆ ◆ ◆

The woman brings her young daughter to the porch. The girl also waves to the engineer each day. As the years pass, the girl grows up.

The engineer grows old and gray during these twenty years. His own children have also grown up.

He has seen terrible tragedies on the tracks. One time, his train hit a wagon full of children. Another time a cheap car stalls on the tracks. The people inside are so frightened that they cannot move. Once an old, deaf hobo is walking along the tracks. He does not hear the warning whistle.

◆ ◆ ◆

But no matter what peril or tragedy he had known, the vision of the little house and the women waving to him with a brave free motion of the arm had become fixed in the mind of the engineer as something beautiful and enduring, something beyond all change and ruin, and something that would always be the same, no matter what <u>mishap</u>, grief or error might break the iron schedule of his days.

◆　◆　◆

Wolfe goes on to say that the engineer has tender feelings toward the women and their house. He makes up his mind that someday he will go and visit them.

At last that day comes. The engineer is retired. He has no more work to do. He rides the train to the town where the women live. He walks through the station and out into the town. As he does this, he begins to feel strange. It doesn't seem like the same town he saw from the train. He becomes more and more puzzled as he walks on. The engineer walks down the hot and dusty road until he gets to the house. The experience seems more and more like a bad dream. He knocks at the door. Then he hears the steps from inside. Finally, the door opens. The woman stands before him.

◆　◆　◆

And instantly, with a sense of bitter loss and grief, he was sorry he had come. He knew at once that the woman who stood there looking at him with a mistrustful eye was the same woman who had waved to him so many thousand times. But her face was harsh and pinched and <u>meager</u>; the flesh sagged wearily in <u>sallow</u> folds, and the small eyes peered at him with timid suspicion and uneasy doubt. All the brave freedom, the warmth and the affection that he had read into her gesture, vanished in the moment that he saw her and heard her unfriendly tongue.

◆　◆　◆

Vocabulary Development

mishap (MIS hap) *n.*　accident
meager (MEE ger) *adj.*　having little flesh, thin
sallow (SAL loh) *adj.*　sickly, pale yellow

◆ **Reading Strategy**

How does the engineer feel about the woman and the house? Based on his feelings, **predict** what will happen next.

_____

_____

_____

_____

_____

◆ **Reading Check**

How does the man feel as he walks toward the house?

_____

_____

_____

_____

_____

The man is disappointed when he meets the woman because she looks at him

_____.

Her face is

_____.

Her eyes are filled with

_____.

He had thought she was warm and friendly, but

_____.

◆ Stop to Reflect

Imagine that you are the mother or the daughter. Do you think their reaction to the man is normal? Explain why you feel as you do.

_____

_____

_____

Wolfe describes how the man explains why he came. The woman finally invites him in, but she seems unwilling to do so. She calls to her daughter in a harsh, shrill voice. They have a short visit in the women's ugly little parlor. As the man tries to talk, the women stare at him in a dull way. They seem hostile and afraid.

The engineer feels disappointed and leaves the cottage. He suddenly feels old and sad. The things that he thought he knew were not the way he expected them to be.

◆   ◆   ◆

And he knew that all the magic of that bright lost way, the vista of that shining line, the imagined corner of that small good universe of hope's desire, was gone forever, could never be got back again.

1. Describe the cottage that the engineer sees from the train. Include the names of four kinds of plants that grow by the cottage.

_____

_____

2. What happened every day just after two o'clock for twenty years? Complete this sequence chart for your answer.

First,

↓

Then,

↓

Then,

↓

After that,

3. Before he retired, the engineer thought of the women as something special. Put a check by each of the four words he might have used to describe them.

____ beautiful   ____ tragic

____ enduring   ____ warm

____ mistrustful   ____ affectionate

____ harsh   ____ unfriendly

4. In the beginning of the story, the engineer has a certain attitude toward the women. This attitude tells something about his own character. How would you describe the character of the engineer?

_____

_____

5. **Literary Analysis:** How do you know that the engineer's meeting with the women is the **anticlimax** of the story?

_____

_____

6. **Reading Strategy:** Thomas Wolfe includes details that help you **predict** the ending. Put a check in front of the three details that prepare you for the ending.

_____ The house was white with green blinds.

_____ The engineer blew the train's whistle every day at the same time.

_____ A woman and her daughter waved as the train passed.

_____ The engineer thought that the women would always stay the same.

_____ The engineer begins to think that he knows the women well.

_____ The woman has an unfriendly tone when she answers the door.

Writing

Comparison-and-Contrast Sentences

The engineer thought the women were one way, but they turned out to be another way. On separate paper, write three sentences in which you compare and contrast the two views of the women. Your sentences may have the following topics:
- What the women look like
- How friendly the women are
- How the women's attitude makes the engineer feel

You may write your own sentences, or you may complete these sentences.

1. The engineer thought the women would look _____, but they turned out to look _____.

2. The engineer thought the women would be _____, but they turned out to be _____.

3. The engineer thought his visit would make him feel _____, but it made him feel _____.

In Another Country

Ernest Hemingway

Summary

In this short story, an American officer who is recovering from a war injury meets four other wounded men: three young Italian officers and an older major. The major helps the American with his Italian grammar, advises him not to marry, and mourns the death of his own wife.

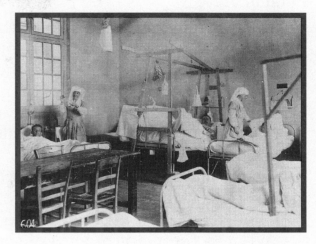

Visual Summary

Characters		
Narrator	Major	Another boy with no nose
Doctor	Three boys	

Setting
A hospital in Milan during World War I

Problem
The characters have been wounded in the war.

1: The doctor tells the narrator that the narrator will play football again in spite of his wound.

2: The doctor tells the wounded major that his withered hand will grow.

3: The major says he is not confident that his hand will get better.

4: The narrator and the boys have the same medals.

5: The narrator worries about how things will be when he goes back to the front.

6: The major and the narrator work on Italian grammar together.

7: One day the major tells the narrator that he must not marry.

8: It turns out that the major's wife has died unexpectedly. The major cries and leaves the hospital.

9: The major returns after three days. In that time, the doctor has put up pictures of completely restored hands. The major, however, only looks out the window.

LITERARY ANALYSIS

Point of View

The **point of view** is the "eyes" through which a story is told. Stories can be told from the **first-person point of view.** In such a story, the narrator uses the pronouns *I, me, we,* and the like. The narrator can be the main character or a minor character in the story.

Stories can be told from the **limited third-person point of view.** In such a story, the speaker telling the story does not use the pronoun *I.* The speaker tells the events of the story and also gets into the mind of one of the characters.

As you read, look for answers to these questions:

- What is the point of view of the story?
- Is the narrator the main character or a minor character in the story?

READING STRATEGY

Identifying with Characters

Characters in stories might have experiences that are different from yours. However, you will find that you share many of their feelings and emotions. When you **identify with characters,** you see what you have in common with them.

As you read, compare your own experiences and feelings with the characters in the story. Keep track in this chart.

Sentence from Story	My Own Feelings
Example: The narrator has been injured in the war.	It would be very scary to be injured in a war, but it would be a relief to get away from the fighting.

In Another Country
Ernest Hemingway

The story opens in Milan, Italy, during World War I. The narrator has been injured in the war. He and the other wounded men do not go to the front anymore. Instead, they go to a hospital for treatment every afternoon. There, they are treated with new machines that are supposed to help them heal.

The doctor approaches the narrator and asks him what he did before the war.

◆　◆　◆

Did you practice a sport?"
I said: "Yes, football."
"Good," he said. "You will be able to play football again better than ever."

◆　◆　◆

The narrator tells about another patient, a major. The major's hand is being treated in a machine. Before the war, the man had been the greatest fencer in Italy. The doctor shows the major a picture of a hand that had been almost as small as the major's. He also shows him a picture of the same hand after treatment. In the second picture, the hand is a little larger.

The major asks if the hand in the picture had been wounded.

◆　◆　◆

"An industrial accident," the doctor said.
"Very interesting, very interesting," the major said, and handed it back to the doctor.
"You have confidence?"
"No," said the major.

◆　◆　◆

◆ **Reading Strategy**

Identify with the narrator, or put yourself in his place. How would you feel about what the doctor says in the underlined sentence?

_____

_____

_____

◆ **Reading Strategy**

Identify with the major. Why does he tell the doctor he has no confidence?

_____

_____

_____

_____

Vocabulary Development

confidence (KAHN fuh duhns) *n.*　being sure, being certain

Other patients include three boys from Milan. Sometimes, when they are done with the machines, they walk to a nearby café. They are sometimes joined by another boy. He wears a black silk handkerchief across his face because he has no nose. He was injured within an hour of going to the front line for the first time.

He doesn't have any medals because he hasn't been in the service long enough. One boy, who was to be a lawyer, has three medals because he had a dangerous job. The rest of the boys and the narrator each have one medal. They are all dealing with death.

◆ ◆ ◆

We were all a little detached, and there was nothing that held us together except that we met every afternoon at the hospital.

◆ ◆ ◆

The narrator says that the boys once asked him what he had done to get his medals. He shows them the papers, which were full of pretty words. But all they really say was that he had gotten the medals because he was an American. After that, the boys act differently toward the narrator. He is still their friend, especially against outsiders. But he is never really one of them after that. It was different with the three Italian boys. They had really earned their medals.

The narrator had been wounded but agrees that it was an accident.

◆ ◆ ◆

I was never ashamed of the ribbons, though, and sometimes, after the cocktail hour, I would imagine myself having done all the things they had done to get their medals; but walking home at night through the empty streets with the cold wind and all the shops closed, trying to keep near the street lights, I knew that I would never have done such things, and I was very much afraid to die, and often lay in bed at night by myself, afraid to die and wondering how I would be when I went back to the front again.

◆ ◆ ◆

The major, the former fencer, does not believe in bravery. He spends a lot of time correcting the narrator's Italian grammar as they sit in the machines. The narrator had once said that Italian seemed like such an easy language. But then the major starts helping him with the grammar. Soon Italian seems so hard that the narrator is afraid to speak until he has the grammar straight in his mind.

The major comes to the hospital every day. He doesn't believe in the machines but feels that they must be tested.

◆ ◆ ◆

It was an idiotic idea, he said, "a theory, like another." I had not learned my grammar, and he said I was a stupid impossible disgrace, and he was a fool to have bothered with me.

◆ ◆ ◆

© Pearson Education, Inc.

In Another Country **155**

◆ **Literary Anaylsis**

A story in the first-person **point of view** gives the thoughts of the narrator. What are the narrator's thoughts about death?

_____

_____

_____

_____

◆ **Literary Analysis**

Mark the Text

Circle all the words in the bracketed paragraph that tell you the story is written from the first-person **point of view.**

The narrator and the major then start talking. The major asks if the narrator is married. The narrator says no, but he hopes to be. The major says that a man must not marry. When asked to explain, he says that a man should not place himself in a position to lose. Instead, he should find things he cannot lose. He speaks with anger and bitterness. The narrator speaks up.

◆   ◆   ◆

"But why should he necessarily lose it?"

"He'll lose it," the major said. He was looking at the wall. Then he looked down at the machine and jerked his little hand out from between the straps and slapped it hard against his thigh. "He'll lose it," he almost shouted. "Don't argue with me!"

◆   ◆   ◆

The major then asks the attendant to turn off the machine. He goes to the other room for more treatment. Then he asks the doctor if he can use the phone. When he returns, he comes toward the narrator and puts his arm on his shoulder.

◆   ◆   ◆

"I am so sorry," he said, and patted me on the shoulder with his good hand. "I would not be rude. My wife has just died. You must forgive me."

"Oh—" I said, feeling sick for him. "I am so sorry."

He stood there biting his lower lip. "It is very difficult," he said. "I cannot <u>resign</u> myself."

Vocabulary Development

resign (ree ZĪN) v. to accept one's fate

He looked straight past me and out through the window. Then he began to cry. "I am <u>utterly</u> unable to resign myself," he said and choked. And then crying, his head up looking at nothing, carrying himself straight and soldierly, with tears on both his cheeks and biting his lips, he walked past the machines and out the door.

◆　◆　◆

The doctor tells the narrator that the major's young wife had died of pneumonia. She had been sick for only a few days. No one thought she would die. The major stays away from the hospital for three days. When he comes back, he is wearing a black band on his sleeve.[2] Now there are large photographs on the wall of before-and-after pictures of wounds cured by the machines. There are three photographs of hands like the major's, completely cured.

◆　◆　◆

I do not know where the doctor got them. I always understood we were the first to use the machines. The photographs did not make much difference to the major because he only looked out of the window.

◆ Read Fluently

Read aloud the bracketed paragraph. Then describe how the major walked out of the hospital.

_____

_____

_____

◆ Reading Check

How long had the major's wife been sick?

_____

_____

_____

◆ Reading Strategy

Identify with the character of the major. What do you think he is thinking about as he looks out the window?

1. _____

2. _____

Vocabulary Development

utterly (UT er lee) *adv.* completely

---

2. **a black band on his sleeve** a sign of mourning.

1. Why do the narrator and the other men go to the hospital every day?

   _____

   _____

2. Write the kind of injury each of these characters has:

   the narrator _____

   the major _____

   the boy with the black handkerchief _____

3. How are the characters being treated for their injuries?

   _____

   _____

4. **Literary Analysis:** Put a check in front of each sentence or passage that tells you the story is written from the first-person **point of view.**

   ____ The major's hand had been injured.

   ____ We all had the same medals . . .

   ____ I had been wounded, it was true . . .

   ____ The major came very regularly to the hospital.

   ____ "Oh—" I said, feeling sick for him.

5. **Reading Strategy:** The narrator says he is afraid to die. He often lies in bed thinking about it and wondering how he will act when he goes back to the front. **Identify with** the narrator. If you were in his place, how would you feel about being on the front?

   _____

   _____

Speaking and Listening

Continue the Story

Write a paragraph that tells what happens next. Before you write, answer these questions:

- Do the major and the narrator stay in touch with each other?

_____

_____

_____

- Does the major's hand get better?

_____

_____

_____

- How does the major deal with his grief?

_____

_____

_____

- Does the narrator go back to the front?

_____

_____

_____

- What happens to the boy whose face was injured?

_____

_____

_____

In one paragraph, you can probably not answer all these questions. Choose one or more ideas, and develop a paragraph. Then, share your paragraph with the class.

A Worn Path

Eudora Welty

Summary

In this short story, an old woman makes her way from her home to Natchez. She walks through woods and fields, along a country path and along a road. When she gets to town, she goes to a doctor's office to get medicine for her grandson. She has been taking care of him since he swallowed lye several years before.

Visual Summary

Sequence of Events			
1.	**2.**	**3.**	**4.**
In December, Phoenix Jackson walks through the pine woods.	She speaks to the wild animals and tells them to keep out of her path.	She walks up and down hills, and at one point she catches her dress in a thorny bush.	She crosses a creek, crawls through a barbed-wire fence, and sees a scarecrow.
5.	**6.**		**7.**
On the road, a dog surprises her and she falls. A hunter helps her up, and a nickel falls out of his pocket. She picks it up.	Phoenix reaches Natchez. She finds the medicine for her grandson, who had swallowed lye several years before. The attendant gives her another nickel.		She plans to buy her grandson a paper windmill before she walks back home.

LITERARY ANALYSIS
Point of View and Narrator

Every story is told by a **narrator**. Some stories are told from the **first-person point of view.** In these stories, the narrator refers to himself or herself as *I*. The narrator also has a role in the events. The narrator's role can be major or minor.

Other stories are told from the **limited third-person point of view.** In these stories, the narrator stands outside the action. The narrator is an outside observer who does not use the pronoun *I*. The narrator might tell the thoughts of one or more characters.

As you read, look for answers to these questions:
- From what point of view is the story told?
- Which character's thoughts does the narrator reveal?

READING STRATEGY
Identifying with Characters

Many stories tell about characters you might never meet. Still, you might see that you have feelings and emotions that are the same as those of the characters. When you notice what you have in common with story characters, you are **identifying with the characters.**

As you read, ask yourself how you would feel if you were in the character's place.

Sentence from Story	My Own Feelings
Example: Far out in the country there was an old Negro woman with her head tied in a red rag, coming along a path through the pinewoods.	I enjoy walking along woodland paths. I like to hear the birds chirping, and I enjoy the fresh smells of the trees.

In mythology, the Phoenix is a special bird. It lives a hundred years, is burned, and rises from the ashes to live again. Why do you think the author named her character Phoenix?

_____

_____

_____

Identify with Phoenix. Why do you think she talks to the animals as she walks through the woods?

_____

_____

_____

A Worn Path
Eudora Welty

An old Negro woman named Phoenix Jackson leaves home on a cold December morning. She walks along a country path.

◆　◆　◆

She was very old and small and she walked slowly in the dark pine shadows, moving a little from side to side in her steps, with the balanced heaviness and lightness of a <u>pendulum</u> in a grandfather clock.

◆　◆　◆

The woman carries a cane that she taps as she walks.

Welty tells us that Phoenix's eyes are blue with age. Her skin is quite wrinkled. Her hair comes down in ringlets from under the red rag.

The woman notices some movement in the bushes.

◆　◆　◆

Old Phoenix said, "Out of my way, all you foxes, owls, beetles, jack rabbits, coons and wild animals! . . . Keep out from under these feet, little bobwhites. . . . Keep the big wild hogs out of my path. Don't let none of those come running my direction. I got a long way."

◆　◆　◆

Phoenix comes to a hill. She climbs up one side of the hill and down the other. On the way, a bush catches her dress. It takes her a long time to get her dress free. She crosses a creek by walking across a log with her eyes closed.

Vocabulary Development

pendulum (PEN dyoo luhm) _n._　a weight hanging from a fixed point so as to swing freely under the action of gravity

---

Phoenix is pleased with herself. She sits down to get comfortable and rest.

◆ ◆ ◆

Up above her was a tree in a pearly cloud of mistletoe. She did not dare to close her eyes, and when a little boy brought her a plate with a slice of marble cake on it she spoke to him. "That would be acceptable," she said. But when she went to take it there was just her own hand in the air.

◆ ◆ ◆

Phoenix keeps on walking. She has to go through a barbed-wire fence. She is very careful. She finally gets through the barbed-wire fence safely. Then she sees a buzzard.[1] She asks him who he's watching. She comes to an old cotton field and then to a field of dead corn. There is no path here. Then she sees something in front of her. It is tall, black, and thin. It is moving.

She sees what she thinks is a man but then is confused by the figure's silence.

◆ ◆ ◆

"Ghost," she said sharply, "who be you the ghost of? For I have heard of nary death close by."

◆ ◆ ◆

The figure moves in the wind but does not answer. She touches its clothes and realizes there is nothing underneath.

◆ ◆ ◆

◆ Literary Analysis

In the bracketed paragraph, what information about Phoenix does the **limited third-person narrator** suggest?

_____

_____

_____

◆ Reading Check

Phoenix sees something in front of her. What does she think it is?

_____

_____

_____

_____

Vocabulary Development

mistletoe (MIS uhl toh) *n.*   a green plant that lives on other plants

nary (NAIR ee) *adj.*   not one

---

1. **sees a buzzard** (BUZ erd) A buzzard is a bird that waits for its prey to die, rather than killing it. Buzzards commonly circle dying prey, so they are seen as a sign of death.

"You scarecrow," she said. Her face lighted. "I ought to be shut up for good," she said with laughter. "My senses is gone. I too old. I the oldest people I ever know. Dance, old scarecrow," she said, "while I dancing with you."

◆ ◆ ◆

Phoenix keeps walking through the corn field. She gets to a wagon track. This is the easy part of the walk. She follows the track. She goes past bare fields, past some trees, past some old cabins. The doors and windows are all boarded. They remind Phoenix of old women who are under a spell, just sitting there.

◆ ◆ ◆

◆ Read Fluently

Read the bracketed paragraph. Then underline what Phoenix says.

In a <u>ravine</u> she went where a spring was silently flowing through a hollow log. Old Phoenix bent and drank. "Sweet gum[2] makes the water sweet," she said, and drank more. "Nobody know who made this well, for it was here when I was born."

◆ ◆ ◆

As she walks along the path near a swamp, Phoenix speaks to the alligators. Then, she crosses a road that is shaded by oak trees.

A black dog comes up to Phoenix. He knocks her down, and she falls into a ditch. She cannot get out of it. A young white hunter comes along. He has a dog with him.

Vocabulary Development

ravine (ruh VEEN) *n.* a small narrow valley with steep sides

---

2. **sweet gum** *n.* a tree that has a sweet-smelling juice.

He asks Phoenix what she is doing. She jokes that she is pretending to be an upside-down bug. She needs his help to get up.

◆ ◆ ◆

He lifted her up, gave her a swing in the air, and set her down. "Anything broken, Granny?"

"No sir, them old dead weeds is springy enough," said Phoenix, when she had got her breath. "I thank you for your trouble."

◆ ◆ ◆

The man asks Phoenix where she lives and where she's going. She tells him she's on her way to town. He tells her that's too far. He says she should just go back home.

Phoenix doesn't move.

◆ ◆ ◆

The deep lines in her face went into a fierce and different <u>radiation</u>. Without warning, she had seen with her own eyes a flashing nickel fall out of the man's pocket onto the ground.

◆ ◆ ◆

Phoenix distracts the man. She cries and claps her hands. She tells the black dog to get away. She whispers, "Sic him!"[3] The man tells Phoenix to watch how he gets rid of the dog. He tells his own dog, "Sic him!" The man runs and throws sticks at the black dog. Phoenix uses this time to pick up the nickel. She slowly bends down.

◆ ◆ ◆

◆ **Reading Check**

How does Phoenix get out of the ditch?

_____

_____

_____

_____

◆ **Literary Analysis**

What detail in the bracketed paragraph tells you that the **narrator** is getting into Phoenix's mind? Underline the sentence that gives the answer.

Vocabulary Development

radiation (ray dee AY shuhn) *n.* arrangement from the center to the sides

---

3. **"Sic him!"** a command given to a dog to attack.

In the bracketed paragraph, do you think Phoenix did something wrong? Write *yes* or *no.* _____

Identify with Phoenix. What would you have done?

_____

_____

_____

Her chin was lowered almost to her knees. The yellow palm of her hand came out from the fold of her apron. Her fingers slid down and along the ground under the piece of money with the grace and care they would have in lifting an egg from under a setting hen. Then she slowly straightened up, she stood erect, and the nickel was in her apron pocket. A bird flew by. Her lips moved. "God watching me the whole time. I come to stealing."

◆ ◆ ◆

The man comes back. He tells Phoenix that he scared the dog off. Then he points the gun at Phoenix. She just stands straight, facing him. He asks her if the gun scares her.

◆ ◆ ◆

"No, sir, I seen plenty go off closer by, in my day, and for less than what I done," she said, holding <u>utterly</u> still.

◆ ◆ ◆

The man admires her bravery. He would give her some money if he had any. He advises her to stay home to be safe. She tells him she has to continue her journey.

The man and Phoenix go in different directions. Phoenix keeps walking. At last she gets to Natchez.[4] The city is decorated for Christmas. Phoenix sees a lady who is carrying an armful of wrapped gifts. Phoenix asks the woman to tie her shoelaces. She says that

---

Vocabulary Development

utterly (UT er lee) *adv.* completely

---

4. **Natchez** (NACH iz): a town in southern Mississippi.

untied shoes are fine for the country. But they don't look right in a big building. Phoenix goes into a big building. She says "Here I be" to the woman at the counter. The woman asks Phoenix for her name, but Phoenix does not answer. The woman asks if Phoenix is deaf. Then the nurse comes in.

◆ ◆ ◆

"Oh, that's just old Aunt Phoenix," she said. "She doesn't come for herself—she has a little grandson. She makes these trips just as regular as clockwork. She lives away back off the Old Natchez Trace."[5] She bent down. "Well, Aunt Phoenix, why don't you just take a seat? We won't keep you standing after your long trip."

◆ ◆ ◆

Phoenix sits down. The nurse asks her about her grandson. She wants to know if his throat is any better. At first, Phoenix does not answer. The nurse asks if the boy is dead. At last, Phoenix answers. She tells the nurse that her memory had left her. She had forgotten why she had come. The nurse wonders how she could forget, after coming so far.

◆ ◆ ◆

"Throat never heals, does it?" said the nurse, speaking in a loud, sure voice to old Phoenix. By now she had a card with something written on it, a little list. "Yes. Swallowed lye. When was it?—January—two-three years ago—"

Phoenix spoke unasked now. "No, missy, he not dead, he just the same. Every little while his throat begin to close up again, and he not able to swallow. He not get his breath. He not able to

Vocabulary Development

lye (Lī) *n.* a strong chemical used in making soap

5. **the Old Natchez Trace** a trace is an old path or trail left by people, animals, or vehicles.

The narrator has waited until now to tell the reason for Phoenix's journey. Would you rather have known earlier? Write *yes* or *no,* and then explain your opinion.

_____

_____

_____

◆ Reading Strategy

Identify with the nurse. Why does she give Phoenix a nickel? Give two reasons.

1.

_____

2.

_____

◆ Reading Check

What does Phoenix plan to buy for her grandson? Circle the answer to the question.

help himself. So the time come around, and I go on another trip for the <u>soothing</u> medicine."

"All right. The doctor said as long as you came to get it, you could have it," said the nurse. "But it's an <u>obstinate</u> case."

◆ ◆ ◆

Phoenix talks about her grandson. She says that they are the only two left in the world. The boy suffers, but he is going to last. He is a sweet boy. The nurse then gives Phoenix the medicine. She says "Charity" as she makes a mark in a book. The nurse gives Phoenix a nickel out of her purse for Christmas. Phoenix takes the other nickel out of her pocket and looks at both of them.

She taps her cane to announce her plan. She is going to buy a paper windmill for her grandson. He has never seen one.

◆ ◆ ◆

She lifted her free hand, gave a little nod, turned around, and walked out of the doctor's office. Then her slow step began on the stairs, going down.

Vocabulary Development

soothing (SOO thing) *adj.* comforting

obstinate (AHB stuh nuht) *adj.* stubborn, not easily changed

1. What time of year is it when Phoenix takes her journey?

_____

2. Put a check by four words that tell what Phoenix Jackson looks like.

____ small   ____ blue-eyed

____ tall   ____ dark-eyed

____ young   ____ wrinkled

____ old   ____ gray-haired

3. What is the purpose of Phoenix's journey?

_____

_____

_____

4. **Literary Analysis:** Put a check in front of each sentence or passage that tells you the story is written from the **limited third-person point of view.**

____ Far out in the country there was an old Negro woman with her head tied in a red rag, coming along a path through the pinewoods.

____ But when she went to take it there was just her own hand in the air.

____ I ought to be shut up for good.

____ I come to stealing.

____ "The doctor said as long as you came to get it, you could have it," said the nurse.

5. **Reading Strategy:** Identify with Phoenix. How important is her grandson to her? Explain how you know.

_____

_____

_____

Writing

Memorial Speech

Imagine that Phoenix Jackson has died. On separate paper, write the speech you might give at her memorial service. In your speech, talk about the good things she did in her life. Also include information about her character.

Prewriting   Reread the story and take notice of details about Phoenix. Look for evidence that she is strong, determined, and brave. Find clues that she has a good sense of humor. Look for proof that she is generous and unselfish.

Drafting   To begin, identify Phoenix Jackson. Explain the sad occasion for the speech. Organize your ideas in order of importance.

Revising   Reread your speech to make sure it shows what kind of person Phoenix was. Change words that are too vague. Add details that will make your audience feel emotional about Phoenix. Write your final speech on a separate sheet of paper.

The First Seven Years
Bernard Malamud

Summary

In this short story, Feld, a shoemaker, wants his nineteen-year-old daughter, Miriam, to go out with a local college boy named Max. One day Max brings in some shoes for repair. Feld persuades him to ask Miriam out. When Max leaves, Sobel, Feld's helper, breaks the last, or the block for repairing shoes, with his heavy pounding. Then he runs out of the shop. Feld hires a new helper who is less trustworthy. After their second date, Miriam reports that Max is a bore without a soul. When Feld finds out that his new helper has been stealing from him, he has a heart attack. When he recovers, he goes to see Sobel. He finds out that Sobel has worked for him for five years only because he is in love with Miriam. Feld asks Sobel to wait two more years before asking Miriam to marry him. The next morning, Sobel is back at work.

Visual Summary

TIMELINE			
Feld wants his daughter, Miriam, to go to college, but she isn't interested.	Feld asks Max, a local college student, to call Miriam.	Feld's assistant, Sobel, breaks the last and rushes out of the store.	Miriam says Max has no soul and she will not see him again.
Feld's new assistant steals from him. Feld is so upset he has a mild heart attack.	Feld asks Sobel to come back to work. He discovers that Sobel has been working for Feld only because of Miriam.	Feld asks Sobel to wait two years before asking Miriam to marry him.	

LITERARY ANALYSIS

Epiphany

An **epiphany** (ee PIF uh nee) is a moment when a character has a sudden insight.

- This insight changes how characters view themselves, other characters, or story events.
- It forms the story's climax, or the high point of interest or suspense.
- It may or may not resolve the conflict in the story.

In "The First Seven Years," the events in the story lead up to the main character's epiphany.

<u>Feld had a sudden insight</u>. In some devious way, with his books and commentary, Sobel had given Miriam to understand that he loved her.

READING STRATEGY

Identifying with Characters

When you **identify with characters** in a story, you connect what they think, feel, say, and do to your own experience. Identifying with characters helps you understand who the characters are and why they act as they do.

As you read, complete this chart. Connect the thoughts, feelings, and actions of a character in the story with your own experience.

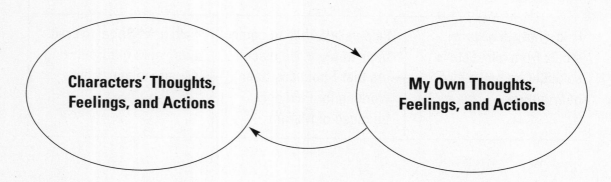

Characters' Thoughts, Feelings, and Actions

My Own Thoughts, Feelings, and Actions

The First Seven Years
Bernard Malamud

Feld is a shoemaker who came to
America from Poland. He has a helper named
Sobel. Feld wishes that his daughter, Miriam,
would go to college. Miriam enjoys reading
books that Sobel lends her, but she would
rather work than go to school. Feld admires a
college student named Max because he has
worked hard to get an education.

◆ ◆ ◆

A figure emerged from the snow and the door
opened. At the counter the man withdrew
from a wet paper bag a pair of battered shoes
for repair. Who he was the shoemaker for a
moment had no idea, then his heart trembled
as he realized, before he had thoroughly
<u>discerned</u> the face, that Max himself was
standing there, embarrassedly explaining what
he wanted done to his old shoes. Though Feld
listened eagerly, he couldn't hear a word, for
the opportunity that had burst upon him was
deafening.

◆ ◆ ◆

Feld would like Max to date his daughter.
He is afraid to suggest the idea. He does not
know whether Max would agree or whether
Miriam would be angry with him. Feld
decides that there is no harm in bringing the
idea up. If his daughter will not think about
going to college herself, Feld wants her to
marry an educated man. He wants her to have
a better life.

Vocabulary Development

discerned (di SERND) *v.* perceived or recognized; made
out clearly

Max describes to Feld what he wants done to his shoes. Then he asks about the price. Before answering, Feld asks Max to step into the hall for a conversation.

◆ ◆ ◆

"Ever since you went to high school," he said, in the dimly-lit hallway, "I watched you in the morning go to the subway to school, and I said always to myself, this is a fine boy that he wants so much an education."

"Thanks," Max said, nervously alert. He was tall and grotesquely thin, with sharply cut features, particularly a beak-like nose. He was wearing a loose, long slushy overcoat that hung down to his ankles, looking like a rug draped over his bony shoulders, and a soggy, old brown hat, as battered as the shoes he had brought in.

"I am a business man," the shoemaker abruptly said to conceal his embarrassment, "so I will explain you right away why I talk to you. I have a girl, my daughter Miriam—she is nineteen—a very nice girl and also so pretty that everybody looks on her when she passes by in the street. She is smart, always with a book, and I thought to myself that a boy like you, an educated boy—I thought maybe you will be interested sometime to meet a girl like this." He laughed a bit when he had finished and was tempted to say more but had the good sense not to.

◆ **Reading Strategy**

Identify with Max, or put yourself in his place. Circle one word or phrase in this paragraph that shows how Max feels during his conversation with Feld.

◆ **Reading Check**

What hope does Feld hold for Miriam and the college boy Max?

_____

_____

_____

Vocabulary Development

grotesquely (groh TESK lee) *adv.* absurdly; strikingly
slushy (SLUHSH ee) *adj.* covered with partly melted snow or ice

Max stared down like a hawk. For an uncomfortable second he was silent, then he asked, "Did you say nineteen?"

"Yes."

"Would it be all right to inquire if you have a picture of her?"

"Just a minute." The shoemaker went into the store and hastily returned with a snapshot that Max held up to the light.

"She's all right," he said.

Feld waited.

"And is she sensible—not the flighty kind?"

"She is very sensible."

After another short pause, Max said it was okay with him if he met her.

◆　◆　◆

Feld gives Max his telephone number. Max puts it away and asks again about the price of the shoes. Feld gives him a price of "a dollar fifty," which is less than he usually charges. Then Feld goes back into the store.

◆　◆　◆

Later, as he entered the store, he was startled by a violent clanging and looked up to see Sobel pounding with all his might upon the naked last.[1] It broke, the iron striking the floor and jumping with a thump against the wall, but before the enraged shoemaker could cry out, the assistant had torn his hat and coat from the hook and rushed out into the snow.

◆　◆　◆

Feld is upset that Sobel has left. He depends on Sobel because he has a heart condition. Sobel, a thirty-year-old Polish refugee, had come looking for work five years before. Now Feld trusts Sobel to run his business but feels guilty because he pays him so poorly. While Sobel does not seem to care about money, he is interested in books.

---

1. **last** *n.* a block shaped like a person's foot, on which shoes are made or repaired.

◆ **Reading Strategy**

Identify with Max. Why does he ask Feld for a picture of Miriam?

_____

_____

_____

_____

◆ **Read Fluently**

Read the bracketed paragraph aloud. Circle three words that reveal how Sobel feels.

◆ Reading Check

How does Feld run his business when Sobel refuses to return to work?

_____

_____

_____

_____

He has loaned books to Miriam and shared his written comments about them with her.

After working alone for a week, Feld goes to Sobel's rooming house to ask him to return. Sobel's landlady tells him that Sobel is not there. Feld is forced to hire a new assistant who is neither as trustworthy nor as skilled as Sobel is. Feld keeps his mind off his problems by thinking about Max and Miriam's first date. He hopes they will like each other.

◆ ◆ ◆

At last Friday came. Feld was not feeling particularly well so he stayed in bed, and Mrs. Feld thought it better to remain in the bedroom with him when Max called. Miriam received the boy, and her parents could hear their voices, his throaty one, as they talked. Just before leaving, Miriam brought Max to the bedroom door and he stood there a minute, a tall, slightly <u>hunched</u> figure wearing a thick, droopy suit, and apparently at ease as he greeted the shoemaker and his wife, which was surely a good sign. And Miriam, although she had worked all day, looked fresh and pretty. She was a large-framed girl with a well-shaped body, and she had a fine open face and soft hair. They made, Feld thought, a first-class couple.

Miriam returned after 11:30. Her mother was already asleep, but the shoemaker got out of bed and after locating his bathrobe went into the kitchen, where Miriam, to his surprise, sat at the table, reading.

"So where did you go?" Feld asked pleasantly.

"For a walk," she said, not looking up.

"I advised him," Feld said, clearing his throat, "he shouldn't spend so much money."

"I didn't care."

Vocabulary Development

hunched (HUNCHT) *adj.* humped over

The shoemaker boiled up some water for tea and sat down at the table with a cupful and a thick slice of lemon.

"So how," he sighed after a sip, "did you enjoy?"

"It was all right."

He was silent. She must have sensed his disappointment, for she added, "You can't really tell much the first time."

"You will see him again?"

Turning a page, she said that Max had asked for another date.

"For when?"

"Saturday."

"So what did you say?"

"What did I say?" she asked, delaying for a moment—"I said yes."

◆   ◆   ◆

Miriam asks her father about Sobel. Feld tells her Sobel has another job. Throughout the week, Feld asks Miriam about Max. He is disappointed when he finds out that Max is taking business classes to become an accountant. Max and Miriam have a second date on Saturday. When Miriam comes home, she tells her father that Max bores her because he is only interested in things. Miriam says Max did not ask her on another date, but she has no interest in going out with him anyway. Feld still hopes that Max will call his daughter again. Instead, Max avoids the shoemaker's shop on his way to school.

One afternoon Max comes to the shop. He pays for his shoes and leaves without saying a word about Miriam. Later that night, Feld has a heart attack after finding out that his new assistant has been stealing from him. Feld stays in bed for three weeks. When Miriam offers to get Sobel, Feld reacts angrily. Once he returns to work, he feels tired. He

Underline two sentences in the bracketed paragraphs that reveal Miriam's reaction to her first date with Max.

◆ Reading Strategy

Identify with Miriam, or put yourself in her position. Why do you think she delays before answering her father's question about a second date with Max?

_____

_____

_____

◆ Reading Strategy

How does Miriam feel about Max after their second date?

_____

_____

_____

realizes he needs Sobel's help. Feld visits Sobel at his rooming house. He notices stacks of books and wonders why Sobel reads so much.

◆ ◆ ◆

"So when you will come back to work?" Feld asked him.

To his surprise, Sobel burst out, "Never."

Jumping up, he strode over to the window that looked out upon the miserable street. "Why should I come back?" he cried.

"I will raise your wages."

"Who cares for your wages!"

The shoemaker, knowing he didn't care, was at a loss what else to say.

"What do you want from me, Sobel?"

"Nothing."

"I always treated you like you was my son."

Sobel <u>vehemently</u> denied it. "So why you look for strange boys in the street they should go out with Miriam? Why you don't think of me?"

The shoemaker's hands and feet turned freezing cold. His voice became so hoarse he couldn't speak. At last he cleared his throat and croaked, "So what has my daughter got to do with a shoemaker thirty-five years old who works for me?"

"Why do you think I worked so long for you?" Sobel cried out. "For the stingy wages I sacrificed five years of my life so you could have to eat and drink and where to sleep?"

"Then for what?" shouted the shoemaker.

"For Miriam," he blurted—"for her."

The shoemaker, after a time, managed to say, "I pay wages in cash, Sobel," and <u>lapsed</u> into silence. Though he was <u>seething</u> with excitement,

---

Vocabulary Development

vehemently (VEE huh ment lee) *adv.* forcefully; intensely
lapsed (LAPST) *v.* passed gradually
seething (SEETH ing) *adj.* boiling

his mind was coldly clear, and he had to admit to himself he had sensed all along that Sobel felt this way. He had never so much as thought it consciously, but he had felt it and was afraid.

"Miriam knows?" he muttered hoarsely.

"She knows."

"You told her?"

"No."

"Then how does she know?"

"How does she know?" Sobel said, "because she knows. She knows who I am and what is in my heart."

Feld had a sudden insight. In some devious way, with his books and commentary, Sobel had given Miriam to understand that he loved her. The shoemaker felt a terrible anger at him for his <u>deceit</u>.

"Sobel, you are crazy," he said bitterly. "She will never marry a man so old and ugly like you."

◆ ◆ ◆

Sobel becomes very angry and then begins to cry. Feld feels sorry for Sobel. He realizes that Sobel barely escaped being killed by the Nazis during World War II and has patiently waited for five years for the girl he loves to grow up. Feld apologizes for calling Sobel ugly. He feels sad when he thinks about the kind of life his daughter will have if she marries Sobel. Feld believes his dreams for a better life for Miriam are dead.

◆ ◆ ◆

"She is only nineteen," Feld said <u>brokenly</u>. "This is too young yet to get married. Don't ask her for two years more, till she is twenty-one, then you can talk to her."

◆ **Reading Check**

How does Sobel feel about Miriam?

_____

_____

_____

◆ **Literary Analysis**

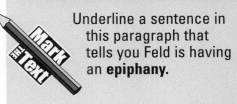

Underline a sentence in this paragraph that tells you Feld is having an **epiphany**.

◆ **Literary Analysis**

How does Feld's **epiphany** change his plans for Miriam?

_____

_____

_____

Vocabulary Development

deceit (duh SEET) *n.* deception; misrepresentation

brokenly (BROH kuhn lee) *adv.* as if crushed by grief

Identify the ambitions that Feld, Miriam, and Sobel have for Miriam's future.

1. _____

_____

_____

2. _____

_____

_____

3. _____

_____

_____

Sobel didn't answer. Feld rose and left. He went slowly down the stairs but once outside, though it was an icy night and the crisp falling snow whitened the street, he walked with a stronger stride.

But the next morning, when the shoemaker arrived, heavy-hearted, to open the store, he saw he needn't have come, for his assistant was already seated at the last, pounding leather for his love.

1. Why is Max so appealing to Feld?

_____

_____

2. How does Miriam feel about Max?

_____

_____

3. Why does Sobel become angry with Feld?

_____

_____

4. How does Miriam feel about Sobel, and why do you think so?

_____

_____

5. **Reading Strategy:** Complete this chart to show the ways in which you **identify with a character** in this story. First, write the name of one character—Feld, Sobel, Max, or Miriam. Next, jot down examples of this character's actions, thoughts, feelings, and situation in the first column. Then list the connections you have to this character in the second column.

Character_____	My Own Experience

6. **Literary Analysis:** What are two changes that take place as a result of Feld's **epiphany?**

1. _____

2. _____

Writing

Personality Profile

What kind of character is Feld, the shoemaker? Refer to the story to find answers to the following questions:
- How does he feel about his daughter?
- How does he act towards his assistant, Sobel?
- What skills does he have?
- What does he value in life?

Use a cluster diagram like the one shown to record details you observe in Feld for a **personality profile.**

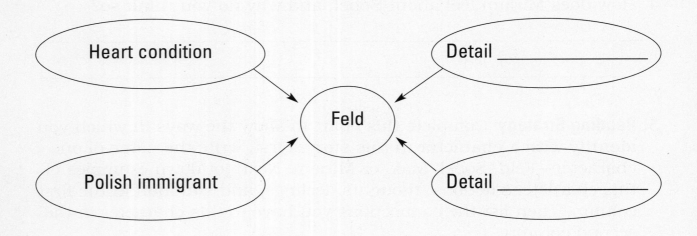

When you finish, share your cluster diagram with a classmate to compare details.

Everyday Use

Alice Walker

Summary

A mother and her daughter Maggie are waiting for a visit from the older daughter, Dee. The mother is a hard-working, undereducated woman who lives in a modest rural home. Maggie is shy and badly scarred from a fire. As they wait, the mother remembers how Dee had hated their poverty. Dee arrives with a long-haired male companion. She asks for some of the family belongings, including two handmade quilts. She wants to display them as pieces of art. The mother snatches the quilts and gives them to Maggie. Dee is angry and leaves with her companion. The story ends with Maggie and her mother sitting happily in the yard.

Visual Summary

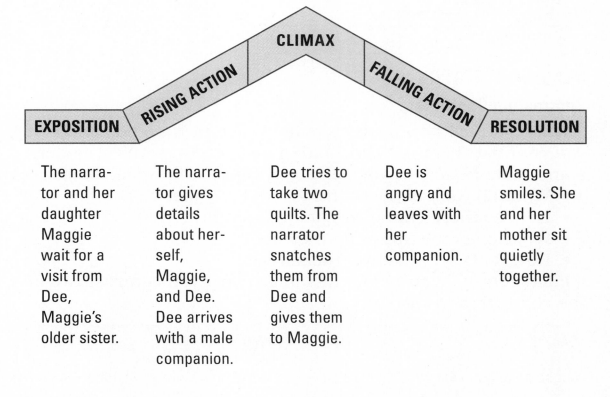

EXPOSITION	RISING ACTION	CLIMAX	FALLING ACTION	RESOLUTION
The narrator and her daughter Maggie wait for a visit from Dee, Maggie's older sister.	The narrator gives details about herself, Maggie, and Dee. Dee arrives with a male companion.	Dee tries to take two quilts. The narrator snatches them from Dee and gives them to Maggie.	Dee is angry and leaves with her companion.	Maggie smiles. She and her mother sit quietly together.

LITERARY ANALYSIS

Character's Motivation

Think of a star athlete. What motivates, or drives, an athlete to play well? Is it pride, a need to win, money, or something else? In a story, a **character's motivation** is the reason behind his or her thoughts, actions, feelings, and words. The reasons that motivate characters might be their values, experiences, needs, or dreams.

In "Everyday Use," Walker gives clues about what motivates characters. In this sentence from the story, Walker hints at why Maggie is embarrassed about the way she looks.

> She has been like this, chin on chest, eyes on ground, feet in shuffle, ever since the fire that burned the other house to the ground.

Use a chart like this one to understand what motivates each character.

Goal or need a character hopes to satisfy ➞	A character's thoughts, actions, feelings, words ➞	Character's motivation

READING STRATEGY

Contrasting Characters

When you tell how characters are different from one another, you contrast them. By **contrasting characters,** you will understand them better. As you read, ask yourself these questions:
- What do each of these characters look like?
- How do these characters act and speak?
- What different values do they hold?
- How do they feel about themselves?

Filling out a diagram like this might help you contrast two of the characters in the story.

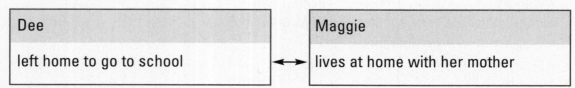

Dee		Maggie
left home to go to school	◄─►	lives at home with her mother

Everyday Use
Alice Walker

The narrator, or storyteller, waits anxiously for her daughter, Dee, to arrive. She knows that her other daughter, Maggie, will be nervous during Dee's visit. Maggie is embarrassed about the burn scars she has on her arms and legs. As she waits, the narrator dreams what it would be like if she and Dee were brought together for a surprise reunion on television. She imagines that Dee hugs her tearfully and pins a beautiful flower on her dress. In this dream, the narrator sees herself as elegant and witty. In reality, she is big, heavy, and strong with rough hands from hard work. She believes Dee would rather have a mother who is thin and has nice skin and hair.

◆ ◆ ◆

"How do I look, Mama?" Maggie says, showing just enough of her thin body enveloped in pink skirt and red blouse for me to know she's there, almost hidden by the door.

"Come out into the yard," I say.

Have you ever seen a lame animal, perhaps a dog run over by some careless person rich enough to own a car, sidle up to someone who is ignorant enough to be kind to him? That is the way my Maggie walks. She has been like this, chin on chest, eyes on ground, feet in shuffle, ever since the fire that burned the other house to the ground.

Vocabulary Development

enveloped (en VEL ohpt) *v.* surrounded

sidle (SĪD ul) *v.* to move sideways in a shy way

◆ **Stop to Reflect**

How is Dee's life different from Maggie's?

_____

_____

_____

_____

◆ **Reading Check**

Why didn't the narrator get an education?

_____

_____

_____

_____

Dee is lighter than Maggie, with nicer hair and a fuller figure. She's a woman now, though sometimes I forget. How long ago was it that the other house burned? Ten, twelve years?

◆　◆　◆

The narrator can still remember the horror of the fire. Maggie was burned terribly.

◆　◆　◆

And Dee. I see her standing off under the sweet gum tree she used to dig gum out of; a look of <u>concentration</u> on her face as she watched the last dingy gray board of the house fall in toward the red-hot brick chimney.

◆　◆　◆

The narrator knows that Dee had hated the house. She wonders why Dee doesn't celebrate as the house burns down.

The narrator remembers how the church helped her raise enough money to send Dee to school in Augusta. The narrator says that Dee always got what she wanted. For example, she got a nice graduation dress and a pair of black shoes to match a suit. In the narrator's opinion, Dee was a stubborn teenager with a mind of her own.

The narrator was not educated. Her school closed after second grade but she doesn't know why. Maggie reads to her, although she struggles because she can't see well.

◆　◆　◆

She knows she is not bright. Like good looks and money, quickness passed her by. She will marry John Thomas (who has mossy teeth in an earnest face) and then I'll be free to sit here and I guess just sing church songs to myself.

◆　◆　◆

Vocabulary Development

concentration (kahn sen TRAY shun) *n.* close, undivided attention

---

The narrator describes her house. It has three rooms, a tin roof, and holes for windows. The narrator believes Dee will hate this house. She says Dee never brought friends to visit. Maggie asks her mother if Dee ever had friends. The narrator remembers a few boys and girls who liked Dee because she was smart.

◆   ◆   ◆

When she comes I will meet—but there they are!

◆   ◆   ◆

Dee and a male friend arrive. Dee wears a flowing yellow and orange dress, long gold earrings, and bracelets. Her friend is short with long hair and a beard. Dee's friend tries to hug Maggie, but she nervously falls back against her mother's chair. While Dee snaps photographs, her mother sits with Maggie behind her. Finally, Dee puts the camera away and kisses her mother on the forehead. Dee's friend tries to shake Maggie's hand, but she doesn't want to.

Dee explains to her mother that her name is now Wangero Leewanika Kemanjo. Her mother wonders what happened to her real name, Dee.

◆   ◆   ◆

"She's dead," Wangero said. "I couldn't bear it any longer, being named after the people who oppress me."

"You know as well as me you was named after your aunt Dicie," I said. Dicie is my sister. She named Dee. We called her "Big Dee" after Dee was born.

"But who was *she* named after?" asked Wangero.

Vocabulary Development

oppress (oh PRES) *v.* keep down by cruel or unjust use of power or authority

---

Why do you think Dee is not **motivated** to bring her friends home?

_____

_____

_____

In the bracketed passage, circle the information about Dee. Underline the information about Maggie. **Contrast** the two **characters**. How do they seem different?

_____

_____

_____

Why has Dee changed her name?

_____

_____

_____

Read the bracketed passage that begins on page 187 aloud. Circle the word that best describes how Dee (Wangero) feels as she speaks.

excited   frustrated

bored   happy

Contrast the characters of Dee and Hakim-a-barber. Explain the different ways that Dee and her friend respond to the dinner they are given.

_____

_____

_____

_____

_____

"I guess after Grandma Dee," I said.

"And who was she named after?" asked Wangero.

"Her mother," I said, and saw Wangero was getting tired.

◆ ◆ ◆

To prevent further discussion, the narrator tells Dee(Wangero) that she doesn't know any more histroy. She actually does.

The narrator talks more about her daughter's new name. Dee (Wangero) tells her mother she does not have to use this name, but the narrator tries to learn how to say it. The narrator also tries to say the name of Dee's friend. She has trouble, so he tells her to call him Hakim-a-barber.

◆ ◆ ◆

We sat down to eat and right away he said he didn't eat collards[1] and pork was unclean. Wangero, though, went on through the chitlins[2] and corn bread, the greens and everything else.

◆ ◆ ◆

Dee (Wangero) loves everything on the table. She even loves the handmade benches they are sitting on. Her daddy had made them because they didn't have money to buy chairs.

Dee (Wangero) tells Hakim-a-barber that she hadn't appreciated the benches until now. She carefully feels the wood.

◆ ◆ ◆

Then she gave a sigh and her hand closed over Grandma Dee's butter dish. "That's it!" she said. "I knew there was something I wanted to ask you if I could have."

◆ ◆ ◆

---

1. **collards** (KAHL erdz) *n.* leaves of the collard plant, often referred to as "collard greens."
2. **chitlins** (CHIT linz) *n.* chitterlings, a pork dish popular among southern African Americans.

Dee (Wangero) asks her mother if she can have the top and handle to an old butter churn. She wants to use the top as a center-piece. Dee (Wangero) asks who made it. Maggie says that their aunt's first husband, Stash, made it. Dee (Wangero) wraps up the pieces to the churn. After dinner, Maggie washes the dishes. Dee (Wangero) looks through a trunk in her mother's room and finds two quilts. Dee's grandmother, mother, and aunt made the quilts from scraps of old dresses and shirts. One quilt pattern is Lone Star. The other is Walk Around the Mountain.

◆ ◆ ◆

"Mama," Wangero said sweet as a bird. "Can I have these old quilts?"
<u>I heard something fall in the kitchen, and a minute later the kitchen door slammed.</u>

◆ ◆ ◆

The narrator offers some other quilts instead. She explains that she made them but Grandma had started them.

◆ ◆ ◆

"No," said Wangero. "I don't want those. They are stitched around the borders by machine."
"That'll make them last better," I said.
"That's not the point," said Wangero. "These are all pieces of dresses Grandma used to wear. She did all this stitching by hand. Imagine!" She held the quilts securely in her arms, stroking them.

◆ ◆ ◆

Dee (Wangero) is still admiring the quilts, but the narrator explains that she has promised them to Maggie as a wedding present.

◆ ◆ ◆

© Pearson Education, Inc.

◆ **Stop to Reflect**

Why do you think Dee wants the pieces to the churn?

_____

_____

_____

◆ **Read Fluently**

Read the underlined sentence aloud. How does Maggie feel about Dee's asking for the quilts?

_____

_____

_____

◆ **Literary Analysis**

Underline two reasons that show why Dee values the quilts and is **motivated** to ask for them.

Mark the Text

◆ **Stop to Reflect**

Dee seems to think that using the quilts for "everyday use" is the wrong way to use them. Do you agree? Why or why not?

_____

_____

_____

_____

◆ **Reading Strategy**

Contrast the two **characters** of Maggie and Dee. How do they differ in their views of the quilts?

_____

_____

_____

_____

_____

◆ **Stop to Reflect**

Do you think Maggie or Dee would better appreciate the quilts? Circle your answer.

Maggie   Dee

Explain your answer.

_____

_____

_____

_____

_____

_____

She gasped like a bee had stung her. "Maggie can't appreciate these quilts!" she said. "She'd probably be backward enough to put them to everyday use."

◆   ◆   ◆

The narrator exclaims that she hopes Maggie will use the quilts. No one has used them all this time while she has saved them. She also remembers that Dee (Wangero) had once told her that the quilts were old-fashioned and that she didn't want to take one to college with her.

◆   ◆   ◆

"But they're *priceless!*" she was saying now, furiously; for she has a temper. "Maggie would put them on the bed and in five years they'd be in rags. Less than that!"

◆   ◆   ◆

Dee (Wangero) becomes angry at the thought of Maggie's having the quilts. The narrator asks Dee (Wangero) what she would do with them. Dee (Wangero) replies that she would hang them on the wall. Maggie listens nearby.

◆   ◆   ◆

"She can have them, Mama," she said, like somebody used to never winning anything, or having anything <u>reserved</u> for her. "I can 'member Grandma Dee without the quilts."

◆   ◆   ◆

The narrator looks at Maggie. She remembers that Maggie learned how to quilt from her grandmother and aunt. She sees that Maggie is slightly afraid of Dee (Wangero) but is not angry.

◆   ◆   ◆

Vocabulary Development

reserved (ree ZERVD) *v.*   kept back or set apart for later use

When I looked at her like that something hit me in the top of my head and ran down to the soles of my feet. Just like when I'm in church and the spirit of God touches me and I get happy and shout. I did something I never had done before: hugged Maggie to me, then dragged her on into the room, snatched the quilts out of Miss Wangero's hands and dumped them into Maggie's lap. Maggie just sat there on my bed with her mouth open.

◆ ◆ ◆

The narrator tells Dee (Wangero) to choose other quilts, but Dee (Wangero) leaves and joins her friend who is waiting in the car. Dee (Wangero) tells the narrator and Maggie that they do not understand their heritage. She also says they are living in the past.

◆ ◆ ◆

She put on some sunglasses that hid every-thing above the tip of her nose and her chin.

Maggie smiled; maybe at the sunglasses. But a real smile, not scared. After we watched the car dust settle I asked Maggie to bring me a dip of snuff.[3] And then the two of us sat there just enjoying, until it was time to go in the house and go to bed.

◆ Literary Analysis

What do you think **motivates** Mama to give Maggie the quilts?

_____

_____

_____

◆ Stop to Reflect

How does Maggie feel after her sister's visit?

_____

_____

_____

---

3. **snuff** (SNUHF) *n.* powdered tobacco.

1. What tragic event happened to Maggie, Dee, and their mother in the past before the story begins?

_____

2. Who comes to visit the narrator and Maggie?

_____

3. A person's heritage includes customs, beliefs, and traditions from the past. List two statements from this story that show Dee's interest in her heritage.

1. _____

2. _____

4. Which character knows more about her heritage? Why do you think so?

_____

5. **Reading Strategy:** Complete this chart to **contrast the characters** of Maggie and Dee.

	Appearance	Attitude	Behavior	Speech
Maggie				
Dee				

6. **Literary Analysis:** What do you think **motivates** the narrator to give the quilts to Maggie? List two reasons.

1. _____

2. _____

Writing

Critical Review

Do you think "Everyday Use" works well as a story? Why, or why not? A **critical review** tells what you think about a short story, poem, or novel. Write down your reactions for a critical review of "Everyday Use."

1. First, write one positive reaction, or something you liked about the story. Think about the characters, the events, and the message the author wants to convey.

   _____

   _____

   Explain why you feel this way.

   _____

   _____

2. Write one negative reaction, or something you did not like about the story.

   _____

   _____

   Tell why you feel this way.

   _____

   _____

3. Now, write a sentence to tell your opinion of the entire story. Tell whether you liked the story or whether you did not like it.

   [Sentence starter] I _____ "Everyday Use."

   Tell why you feel this way. Give reasons to support your opinion.

   [Sentence starter] I _____ the story because _____

   _____

   _____

4. On a separate sheet of paper, finish your critical review. Then read it aloud to share it with your classmates.

Mother Tongue

Amy Tan

Summary

In this essay, Amy Tan talks about "all the good Englishes" she uses as a Chinese American. She begins to think about them one day when her mother attends one of her talks. Tan realizes that she is using a different English in her talk from what she uses when she speaks with her mother. Then she describes a number of times when her mother was treated less politely because of her limited and original English. Even as a child, Tan—whose English is perfect—sometimes had to make phone calls for her mother. Tan wonders whether more Asian Americans become engineers because their parents speak limited English at home. Then Tan explains that when she begins to think of her mother as her reader, she finds her voice as a writer.

Visual Summary

Main Idea

"Language is the tool of my trade. And I use them all—all the Englishes I grew up with."

Supporting Details

Tan realizes that she uses different English in her talks from the English she uses with her mother.	Tan has to make phone calls for her mother. People don't take her mother seriously because her English is limited.	Tan thinks students with parents who speak limited English have trouble with standardized tests.	When Tan decides to imagine a reader for her writing, she picks her mother.

LITERARY ANALYSIS

Reflective Essay

What is a **reflective essay?**
- A **reflective essay** is a short work of nonfiction.
- It tells a writer's personal view of a topic.
- The topic of the essay might be a personal experience or an important event.
- The writer sometimes explores an experience or event to find a deeper meaning.

In "Mother Tongue," Tan shares her thoughts about the English language. In this passage from the essay, Tan, the daughter of a Chinese immigrant, explains why she values the written and spoken word:

> I am a writer. And by that definition, I am someone who has always loved language. I am fascinated by language in daily life. I spend a great deal of my time thinking about the power of language. . . . Language is the tool of my trade.

READING STRATEGY

Evaluating a Writer's Message

In a reflective essay, a writer often explores the meaning of his or her personal experiences. When you read a reflective essay, first identify the message, or main point, the writer is trying to make about these experiences. Then **evaluate a writer's message** by judging whether you do or do not agree with it. Use a chart like the one below to make your evaluation.

On the chart, list facts, reasons, or examples Tan uses to support her views about the challenges faced by people who speak "limited" English. When you finish reading, tell whether you agree or disagree with Tan's message.

Tan's Message	Supporting Evidence	Your Response
People who speak "limited" English are often judged unfairly.	They are not taken seriously by people in department stores, banks, and restaurants.	

Mother Tongue

Amy Tan

◆ Literary Analysis

Underline three words, phrases, or sentences in the bracketed paragraphs that let you know this will be a **reflective essay**.

◆ Reading Check

What makes Tan aware of the "different Englishes" she uses?

_____

_____

_____

_____

I am not a scholar of English or literature. I cannot give you much more than personal opinions on the English language and its variations in this country or others.

I am a writer. And by that definition, I am someone who has always loved language. I am fascinated by language in daily life. I spend a great deal of my time thinking about the power of language—the way it can <u>evoke</u> an emotion, a visual image, a complex idea, or a simple truth. Language is the tool of my trade. And I use them all—all the Englishes I grew up with.

Recently, I was made <u>keenly</u> aware of the different Englishes I do use. I was giving a talk to a large group of people, the same talk I had already given to half a dozen other groups. The nature of the talk was about my writing, my life, and my book, *The Joy Luck Club*.[1] The talk was going along well enough, until I remembered one major difference that made the whole talk sound wrong. My mother was in the room. And it was perhaps the first time she had heard me give a lengthy speech, using the kind of English I have never used with her.

◆ ◆ ◆

Tan realizes that she is using complicated English—the kind of standard English she learned in school.

◆ ◆ ◆

Vocabulary Development

evoke (ee VOHK) *v.* call forth or draw out
keenly (KEEN lee) *adv.* strongly

---

1. **The Joy Luck Club** Amy Tan's highly praised 1989 novel about four Chinese American women and their mothers.

Just last week, I was walking down the street with my mother, and I again found myself conscious of the English I was using, the English I do use with her. We were talking about the price of new and used furniture and I heard myself saying this: "Not waste money that way." My husband was with us as well, and he didn't notice any switch in my English. And then I realized why. It's because over the twenty years we've been together I've often used the same kind of English with him, and sometimes he even uses it with me. It has become our language of intimacy, a different sort of English that relates to family talk, the language I grew up with.

◆ ◆ ◆

Tan shares a conversation she had with her mother, demonstrating what her "family talk" sounds like. When Tan's mother speaks, she does not use Standard English. However, Tan's mother understands more than her limited use of English suggests. For example, Tan's mother follows complicated business and finance news. While Tan's friends do not always completely understand her mother, Tan understands her mother's English because it is what she grew up with. Tan explains that the way her mother speaks English influences the way she views the world.

◆ ◆ ◆

Lately, I've been giving more thought to the kind of English my mother speaks. Like others, I have described it to people as "broken," or "fractured" English. But I <u>wince</u> when I say that. It has always bothered me

◆ Reading Check

How does Tan's language change when she speaks with her mother?

_____

_____

_____

◆ Stop to Reflect

Tan calls the English she grew up with "family talk." Does your family have any words or phrases that would be hard for others to understand?

_____

_____

_____

_____

◆ Literary Analysis

Underline one sentence in this paragraph that points to the fact that this essay is **reflective**.

Vocabulary Development

wince (WINS) *v.* draw back slightly as if in pain

that I can think of no way to describe it other than "broken," as if it were damaged and needed to be fixed, as if it lacked a certain wholeness and soundness. I've heard other terms used, "limited English," for example. But they seem just as bad, as if everything is limited, including people's perceptions of the limited English speaker.

I know this for a fact, because when I was growing up, my mother's "limited" English limited my perception of her. I was ashamed of her English. I believed that her English reflected the quality of what she had to say. That is, because she expressed them imperfectly her thoughts were imperfect. And I had plenty of <u>empirical</u> evidence to support me: the fact that people in department stores, at banks, and at restaurants did not take her seriously, did not give her good service, pretended not to understand her, or even acted as if they did not hear her.

◆   ◆   ◆

Tan explains that her mother herself also realized how her limited use of English created problems. When Tan was fifteen, she was asked to call people to get information for her mother. For example, Tan once called a stockbroker to find out about a missing check. More recently, Tan's mother went to the hospital to learn the results of a brain scan. After the hospital claimed to have lost the scan, Mrs. Tan refused to leave until the doctor called her daughter. Tan arranged to get the information her mother wanted. She also received an apology for the hospital's mistake.

◆   ◆   ◆

Vocabulary Development

empirical (em PEER i kul) *adj.* obtained from observation or experiment

◆ Reading Check

Circle one word or phrase in this paragraph that reveals how Tan used to feel about her mother's use of the English language.

◆ Stop to Reflect

As she was growing up, Tan thought her mother's English reflected the quality of her thoughts. What evidence seemed to support Tan's thoughts?

_____

_____

_____

_____

I think my mother's English almost had an effect on limiting my possibilities in life as well. Sociologists[2] and linguists[3] probably will tell you that a person's developing language skills are more influenced by peers. But I do think that the language spoken in the family, especially in immigrant families which are more insular, plays a large role in shaping the language of the child. And I believe that it affected my results on achievement tests, IQ tests, and the SAT.[4] While my English skills were never judged as poor, compared to math, English could not be considered my strong suit.

◆　◆　◆

Tan did fairly well in English in school. However, she always had higher scores in math and science achievement tests. Tan believes she did well on math tests because there was only one right answer. On the other hand, she had problems with English tests because she felt that the answers depended on personal experience and opinions. Tan could not sort through all the vivid images that came to mind when she tried to answer fill-in-the-blank sentence completions or word analogies.

◆　◆　◆

I have been thinking about all this lately, about my mother's English, about achievement tests. Because lately I've been

◆ **Reading Strategy**

What point about developing language skills is Tan making in the bracketed paragraph? What evidence does Tan give to support her point? To **evaluate the message,** tell whether you agree or disagree with her and why.

_____

_____

_____

_____

_____

◆ **Reading Check**

When Tan took standardized tests, how did she do in English?

_____

_____

_____

_____

Vocabulary Development

insular (IN syoo lahr) *adj.* suggestive of the isolated life of an island

---

2. **sociologists** (SOH see AHL uh jists) *n.* people who study human social behavior.
3. **linguists** (LING gwists) *n.* people who study human speech.
4. **SAT** Scholastic Aptitude Test; national college entrance exam.

Why does Tan think teachers may be steering Asian-American students away from writing?

_____

_____

_____

_____

Read the bracketed paragraph here and on the next page aloud. What four kinds of "Englishes" does Tan use in her writing?

1. _____

2. _____

3. _____

4. _____

asked, as a writer, why there are not more Asian Americans represented in American literature. Why are there few Asian Americans enrolled in creative writing programs? Why do so many Chinese students go into engineering? Well, these are broad sociological questions I can't begin to answer. But I have noticed in surveys—in fact, just last week—that Asian students, as a whole, always do significantly better on math achievement tests than in English. And this makes me think that there are other Asian-American students whose English spoken in the home might also be described as "broken" or "limited." And perhaps they also have teachers who are <u>steering</u> them away from writing and into math and science, which is what happened to me.

◆　◆　◆

Tan describes how she rebelled against Asian-American stereotypes to become a writer. First, she chose to study English rather than science in college. Then she became a freelance writer after an employer told her that she could not write. In 1985 Tan started writing fiction. At first, she wrote difficult sentences to prove she could use English well.

◆　◆　◆

Fortunately, for reasons I won't get into today, I later decided I should <u>envision</u> a reader for the stories I would write. And the reader I decided upon was my mother, because these were stories about mothers. So with this reader in mind—and in fact she did read my early drafts—I began to write stories using all the Englishes I grew up with: the English I spoke

Vocabulary Development

steering (STEER ing) *v.* guiding; directing
envision (en VIZH uhn) *v.* picture in the mind; imagine

to my mother, which for lack of a better term might be described as "simple"; the English she used with me, which for lack of a better term might be described as "broken"; my translation of her Chinese, which could certainly be described as "watered down"; and what I imagined to be her translation of her Chinese if she could speak in perfect English, her internal language, and for that I sought to preserve the essence, but neither an English nor a Chinese structure. I wanted to capture what language ability tests can never reveal: her intent, her passion, her imagery, the rhythms of her speech and the nature of her thoughts.

Apart from what any critic had to say about my writing, I knew I had succeeded where it counted when my mother finished reading my book and gave me her verdict: "So easy to read."

◆ **Stop to Reflect**

What are three words you would use to describe Tan's relationship with her mother?

1. _____

2. _____

3. _____

1. Why is language important to Tan?

   _____

   _____

2. What are two "Englishes" that Tan uses?

   1. _____

   2. _____

3. What are three things that happened to Tan as a result of her mother's use of "limited" English? List them on a chart like this one.

   ```
              ┌─────────────────────┐
              │        Cause        │
              │  Tan's mother does not │
              │ speak Standard English. │
              └─────────────────────┘
              /          │          \
   ┌──────────┐  ┌──────────┐  ┌──────────┐
   │  Effect  │  │  Effect  │  │  Effect  │
   │          │  │          │  │          │
   │          │  │          │  │          │
   └──────────┘  └──────────┘  └──────────┘
   ```

4. What influence do you think Tan's mother has had on her daughter's writing?

   _____

   _____

5. **Literary Analysis:** Name one personal experience Tan explores in this reflective essay.

   _____

   _____

6. **Reading Strategy:** In your own words, restate Tan's message about how people who do not speak Standard English are often treated. Then **evaluate the message** by deciding whether you do or do not agree with it. Explain why you feel this way.

_____

_____

_____

Listening and Speaking

Speech

What challenges did Tan face in becoming a writer? What experiences helped her learn about different uses of English? Write three points that Tan might include in a **speech** for young people who want to become writers.

- Write one main point for your speech.

_____

- Give one fact, reason, or example to support this main point.

_____

- Write another main point.

_____

- Give one fact, reason, or example to support the second main point.

_____

- Write a third main point.

_____

- Give one fact, reason, or example to support your third point.

_____

- Write out the speech on index cards. List each main point and its supporting evidence on a separate card.
- Then practice the speech before giving it to an audience of your classmates.
- When you give the speech, speak slowly and clearly. Remember to make eye contact with your audience.

Part 2

Reading Informational Materials

Part 2 contains the **Reading Informational Materials** features from *Prentice Hall Literature: Timeless Voices, Timeless Themes* with reading support and practice.

- Review the **Reading Informational Materials** page. You will use the information and skills on this page as you read the selection.

- Read the selection and respond to the questions. Look for the **Mark the Text** logo for special help with interactive reading.

- Use the **Reading Informational Materials** questions at the end of each selection to build your understanding of various types of informational materials.

- Use the **Review and Assess** questions at the end of each selection to review what you have read and to check your understanding.

READING INFORMATIONAL MATERIALS

About Web Sites

A **Web site** is a collection of Web pages—text and graphics on a topic that can be found on the Internet. Each page has its own URL, or "address." Web sites feature underlined words that serve as links to other sites or pages. By clicking on these words, you can find more information.

Reading Strategy

Locating Appropriate Information

To get the most out of Internet research, learn how to **locate appropriate information**. To use a search engine, use specific words. For instance, if you are looking for information on the Puritans who settled in America, you might use the word *Pilgrim*. Too broad a term, such as *colony*, will produce a list that is too long.

Even a focused search term may yield too many results. To further narrow down the list of sites, review the name of the sponsor that is listed on the search engine list, along with the brief excerpt from the site.

The box at right lists a few of the features found on Web sites. Not every feature will be appropriate to your search, so keep your purpose in mind as you explore.

Elements of Web Sites

- **Hotspotted text, buttons,** and other **navigation elements** help you move around the site quickly. Click on any area of the page over which your cursor changes to a hand, and you will be brought to a linked page.

- **A SEARCH function** helps you locate information anywhere on the site, using search terms.

- **Photos, videos, and audio clips** enrich many sites. You may need to download additional software to use these resources.

- **Links** connect you to related Web sites.

- **Contact information** tells you who sponsored the site. An e-mail address to which you may send questions or comments may be included.

BUILD UNDERSTANDING

Knowing this term will help you understand the information on this Web site.

virtual tour (VER choo uhl TOOR) a tour that is taken through a computer

http://www.plimoth.org/

◆ **Stop to Reflect**

Web designers work to create home pages that are visually attractive so that visitors will want to explore the sites further. Do you think the designers of this site were successful? _____

Why or why not?

_____

_____

_____

_____

◆ **Reading Web Pages**

The buttons on the left side of the screen are links to other pages on the **Web site**. Circle the link you would click on if you wanted to find out the date of an event at Plimoth Plantation.

◆ **Reading Strategy**

Web sites often provide search engines to help users find **appropriate information**. Circle this Web site's search engine. What information might you search for on this site?

_____

_____

_____

◆ Stop to Reflect

Why do you think the navigation bar, which is bracketed, appears not just on the home page but also on this interior page?

_____

_____

_____

◆ Reading Strategy

Circle the link you would click on if you wanted to **locate information** about the Mayflower II.

Reading Informational Materials

List five key words you could use to access this **Web site**.

1. _____

2. _____

3. _____

4. _____

5. _____

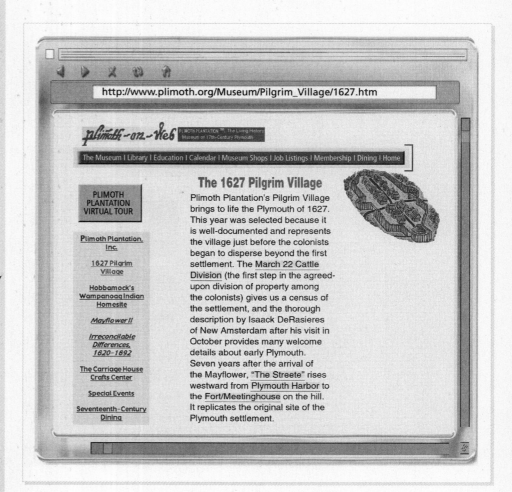

http://www.plimoth.org/Museum/Pilgrim_Village/1627.htm

plimoth-on-web PLIMOTH PLANTATION™: The Living History Museum of 17th-Century Plymouth

The Museum | Library | Education | Calendar | Museum Shops | Job Listings | Membership | Dining | Home

PLIMOTH PLANTATION VIRTUAL TOUR

Plimoth Plantation, Inc.

1627 Pilgrim Village

Hobbamock's Wampanoag Indian Homesite

Mayflower II

Irreconcilable Differences, 1620–1892

The Carriage House Crafts Center

Special Events

Seventeenth-Century Dining

The 1627 Pilgrim Village

Plimoth Plantation's Pilgrim Village brings to life the Plymouth of 1627. This year was selected because it is well-documented and represents the village just before the colonists began to disperse beyond the first settlement. The March 22 Cattle Division (the first step in the agreed-upon division of property among the colonists) gives us a census of the settlement, and the thorough description by Isaack DeRasieres of New Amsterdam after his visit in October provides many welcome details about early Plymouth. Seven years after the arrival of the Mayflower, "The Streete" rises westward from Plymouth Harbor to the Fort/Meetinghouse on the hill. It replicates the original site of the Plymouth settlement.

Check Your Comprehension

1. From the home page, what tool can you use to find Plimoth Plantation's calendar of events without knowing the URL for that page?

_____

2. In the essay "The 1627 Pilgrim Village," why are the words *Plymouth Harbor* and *Fort/Meetinghouse* underlined?

_____

Applying the Reading Strategy

Locating Appropriate Information

3. Using the chart, indicate where you would expect to find the answers to each question—on the home page, the interior page, or in material found through a link.

Question	Location
When will the Holiday Fair at Plimouth be held?	
Do any early documents contain a census of the village?	
Why did the Pilgrims come to North America?	
What purpose or purposes did the Meetinghouse serve?	

Using Informational Materials

What is the value of visiting a site like the one pictured in this lesson instead of reading a book about Plymouth Colony? On the lines below, jot down your ideas about the advantages and disadvantages of Web sites and more traditional reference sources, such as encyclopedias, atlases, and books. Then, on another piece of paper, write a conclusion based on your notes.

_____

_____

About Newspaper Editorials

A **newspaper editorial** is a persuasive essay that addresses a current topic on which public opinion may be divided. It presents the editor's or publisher's point of view. Occasionally, a newspaper may pair two editorials representing opposing points of view, creating a debate of sorts. In the editorials you are about to read, the newspaper presents two opposing viewpoints on the benefits of *pro bono* work—services donated "for the public good."

Reading Strategy

Analyzing Logical and Faulty Modes of Persuasion

To achieve its persuasive purpose, an editorial's argument requires factual support. Such support may include

- *statistics*, or numerical data.
- *anecdotes*, or brief stories, that illustrate the writer's point.
- *quotations* from expert sources.
- *facts* that are well researched and that support the writer's view.

Faulty modes of persuasion, on the other hand, twist facts or use nonfactual methods in an attempt to persuade. *Loaded language*, for example, uses words with strongly negative or positive connotations. Another faulty mode of persuasion is a *bandwagon appeal*, which urges readers to adopt a course of action because "everyone is doing it."

BUILD UNDERSTANDING

Knowing these words will help you read these newspaper editorials.

American Bar Association a voluntary organization of lawyers, judges, law students, and law teachers. Its goals include promoting the administration of justice and upholding high standards of legal education and ethics

pro bono (PROH BOH noh) *n.* from Latin, meaning "for the good"; professional services provided without payment

ethics (ETH iks) *n.* system of morals of a particular person, religion, group, or profession

Lawyers Leave Poor Behind

Our View: Volunteerism in legal profession drops as salaries rise.

◆ **Reading Newspaper Editorials**

This **newspaper editorial** expresses a specific viewpoint. Underline that viewpoint.

1 For weeks, the head of the Arizona Civil Liberties Union has been asking law firms to represent, on a volunteer basis, a client in a free-speech case against the state government. And for weeks, Eleanor
5 Eisenberg has been turned down.

Eisenberg knows firsthand what national statistics are now showing: Law firms are bucking the national trend toward charity and doing less "pro bono" work than in the past. As a result, there aren't
10 enough lawyers willing to represent the poor and disenfranchised[1] when they have legal trouble.

According to a recent survey by *The American Lawyer* magazine, lawyers average 40 minutes of pro bono work per week on lawsuits. That's 35% less
15 unpaid legal work than in 1992.

Lawyers aren't even keeping their own standards. During the same period that 20% more Americans took up volunteer work, attorneys at 82 of the USA's top 100 law firms averaged fewer than the 50 hours a
20 year of pro bono that the American Bar Association (ABA) recommends.

But instead of offering solutions for the disenfran-chised, the bar association gives excuses. ABA pro bono committee chairman Robert Weiner says the
25 top firms' record isn't as bad as it looks, and pre-dicts it will improve as young, idealistic new hires demand to do charitable work and change the cul-ture of their offices.

◆ **Reading Strategy**

In the bracketed section, the writer presents statis-tics. Is this an example of a **logical** or **faulty mode of persuasion**?

_____

Explain.

_____

_____

_____

_____

---

1. disenfranchised (dis in FRAN chīzd) *n.* those who are deprived of privi-leges, rights, and power.

◆ **Read Fluently**

Read the first bracketed paragraph aloud. Then, underline the phrase that supports the writer's claim that many lawyers have been told to spend more time working.

That view glibly skips over the real problem: To cover wildly increasing salaries, lawyers at many firms have been told to work more hours—2,000 per year in some cases—to bring in more revenue, according to findings from the Pro Bono Institute at Georgetown University.

Some firms in Washington, D.C., Texas, and California have stopped or cut back on counting pro bono hours as part of their lawyers' work time, institute president Esther Lardent says. With management creating that sort of an atmosphere, it's no surprise that charitable work at all but a dozen of the nation's biggest firms gets short shrift.

The ABA's own statistics show that 80% of the nation's poor are forced to go without legal help when they really need it. And the association is in the perfect position to lead efforts to ensure that the poor are treated equally.

For a start, it should encourage greater donations to legal-aid charities and insist that pro bono hours be counted as part of a lawyer's performance. A toughly worded rule could influence state bar associations, which often have the power to enforce standards.

Last winter, the Minnesota state bar was defeated in its effort to force lawyers to report fully the amount of pro bono work they do. Similar measures in Massachusetts and Colorado were also defeated.

Yet reforms do work. In Florida, a court forced lawyers to disclose their pro bono hours, and the ABA says their record subsequently improved.

The late Supreme Court Justice Louis Brandeis once noted that the legal profession "is an occupation which is pursued largely for others and not merely for one's self."

The ABA needs to remind law firms of that standard—forcefully.

30

35

40

45

50

55

60

◆ **Reading Newspaper Editorials**

A persuasive piece of writing, such as a **newspaper editorial**, often suggests a specific course of action. What course of action does the writer suggest in the second bracketed section?

_____

_____

_____

_____

◆ **Stop to Reflect**

Do you think that forcing lawyers to disclose their *pro bono* hours will make them work more *pro bono* hours? Explain.

_____

_____

_____

_____

September 25, 2000

Pro Bono Work Still Valued

Opposing View:
Idealistic new lawyers will lead way in boosting service to poor.

By Robert N. Weiner

65 The great judge, Learned Hand, once identified the central commandment in a democracy, "Thou shalt not ration justice." As caretakers of our system of justice, lawyers have a special obligation to ensure access to justice for those who cannot

70 afford legal fees.

The legal profession has embraced its obligation to serve the poor. Our model code of ethics instructs that "A lawyer should aspire to render at least 50 hours of pro bono public legal services per year,"

75 primarily to persons of limited means.

The legal profession can be proud of its record. The recent survey indicating a drop in pro bono hours covers only some large firms, not the profession as a whole. The largest 500 firms donated more

80 than 2 million pro bono hours in 1999. Moreover, the vast majority of lawyers do not practice in large firms. These lawyers, including government attorneys and corporate counsel, also do valuable pro bono work, serving as the last best hope of the

85 least fortunate among us.

◆ **Reading Strategy**

Review the information on p. 210 about **modes of persuasion**. What logical mode of persuasion does the writer use in the opening paragraph?

_____

_____

◆ **Read Fluently**

The writer of this editorial disagrees with the views presented in the first editorial. Read the bracketed paragraph aloud. Then, underline a sentence that supports this opposing view.

Which **logical mode of persuasion** is used in the bracketed paragraph?

_____

_____

Reading Informational Materials

Summarize the view presented in each **newspaper editorial**.

1. _____

_____

2. _____

_____

_____

Which editorial do you find most persuasive?

_____

Explain.

_____

_____

_____

Indeed, many lawyers, from every corner of the profession, have toiled with great dedication on behalf of the poor. The American Bar Association (ABA), for example, launched an effort to obtain representation for disabled children denied Social Security benefits. Thousands of lawyers responded. In addition, with numerous projects ranging from rural pro bono to child custody to immigration and asylum, ABA has worked with state and local programs linking many thousands of lawyers with even more clients.

Nonetheless, we meet less than 20% of the legal needs of the poor, far short of ensuring access to justice. In addition to pro bono efforts, federal funding of the Legal Services Corp. remains critical.

The paradox here is that prosperity—higher billable hours—indeed has put pressure on pro bono time. But this will not last. Firms must compete for the best law students. They remain idealistic, and a prime area of competition is the firms' pro bono programs. We expect that this new generation of lawyers will reinforce our profession's commitment to its most basic values.

Robert N. Weiner is chairman of the American Bar Association's Standing Committee on Pro Bono and Public Service.

Check Your Comprehension

1. According to the first editorial, how well do lawyers meet the standard for *pro bono* work set by the American Bar Association?

   _____

2. According to the second editorial, how should the legal profession feel about its record regarding *pro bono* work?

   _____

Applying the Reading Strategy

Analyzing Logical and Faulty Modes of Persuasion

3. For each editorial, list an example of each of the following persuasive techniques: statistics, quotations, anecdotes.

   Editorial 1: _____

   _____

   Editorial 2: _____

   _____

4. Does either editorial use faulty modes of persuasion? _____
   Explain. _____

   _____

Writing Informational Materials

   Choose an issue that is of importance to you. Then, on a separate piece of paper, write an editorial for your school newspaper about this issue. Make sure that you use several logical modes of persuasion in your editorial. After deciding on your issue, you can ask someone else to write the opposing point of view for the paper.

READING INFORMATIONAL MATERIALS

About Memorandums

A **memorandum** is a business document that tells employees about upcoming events, changes in policy, or other business-related matters. In today's workplace, the average memorandum is brief and informal in tone. It usually contains a heading that indicates the sender, recipient, date, and subject of the memorandum. The body of the memo explains the subject in detail.

Historic memorandums are often more formal, more detailed, and longer than today's memorandums. Look for these qualities in this historic memorandum in which Thomas Jefferson assigned Meriwether Lewis the task of exploring the Missouri River in 1803.

Reading Strategy

Analyzing Text Structures: Patterns of Organization

Informative writing can follow several different **patterns of organization**. Three patterns are described in the chart below.

Pattern of Organization	Structure	Type of writing in which it is often found
Chronological Order	Step-by-step details are presented in time order.	Do-it-yourself instructions
Order of Importance	Ideas flow from most to least important or from least to most important.	Persuasive writing
Enumeration	Supporting details are provided in list form.	Brochures or sales documents

BUILD UNDERSTANDING

Knowing these words will help you read this historic memorandum.

commerce (KAHM ers) *n.* the buying and selling of goods

latitude and longitude east/west and north/south geographic lines that are used to pinpoint any location on Earth's surface

portage (POR tij) *n.* an area of land across which boats must be carried in order to reach the next stretch of open water

Commission of Meriwether Lewis

Thomas Jefferson

June 20, 1803

Historic **memorandums** differ in format but contain the same information as modern memos. Circle the name of the person who received this memorandum. Underline the sender and the date.

1   To Meriwether Lewis, esquire,
captain of the first regiment of
infantry of the United States of
America: Your situation as secretary
5   of the president of the United States,
has made you acquainted with the
objects of my confidential message of
January 18, 1803, to the legislature;
10 you have seen the act they passed,
which, though expressed in general
terms, was meant to sanction those
objects, and you are appointed to
carry them into execution.

. . .

15 The object of your mission is to explore the
Missouri river, and such principal streams of it, as, by
its course and communication[1] with the waters of the
Pacific ocean, whether the Columbia, Oregon [*sic*],
Colorado, or any other river, may offer the most
20 direct and practicable[2] water-communication across
the continent, for the purposes of commerce.
Beginning at the mouth of the Missouri, you will
take observations of latitude and longitude, at all
remarkable points on the river, and especially at the
25 mouths of rivers, at rapids, at islands, and other
places and objects distinguished by such natural
marks and characters, of a durable kind, as that they
may with certainty be recognized hereafter. The

◆ Reading Check

Read the bracketed passage. Then, summarize what you have read by filling in the blanks with your own words.

Lewis's task was to

_____

in order to _____

_____ .

---

1. communication (kuh MYOO ni KAY shun) *n.* the action of passing from one place to another.
2. practicable (PRAK ti kuh bul) *adj.* usable.

◆ Stop to Reflect

List three things that Jefferson wants Lewis to observe.

1. _____

2. _____

3. _____

Why would Lewis's observations be important for future travel and trade?

_____

_____

_____

_____

_____

◆ Reading Check

What does Jefferson suggest that Lewis do when he has leisure time during the journey?

_____

_____

courses of the river between these points of observation may be supplied by the compass, the log-line, and by time, corrected by the observations themselves. The variations of the needle, too, in different places, should be noticed.

The interesting points of the portage between the heads of the Missouri,[3] and of the water offering the best communication with the Pacific Ocean, should also be fixed by observation;[4] and the course of that water to the ocean, in the same manner as that of the Missouri.

Your observations are to be taken with great pains and accuracy; to be entered distinctly and intelligibly for others as well as yourself; to comprehend all the elements necessary, with the aid of the usual tables, to fix the latitude and longitude of the places at which they were taken; and are to be rendered to the war-office, for the purpose of having the calculations made concurrently by proper persons within the United States. Several copies of these, as well as of your other notes, should be made at leisure times, and put into the care of the most trustworthy of your attendants to guard, by multiplying them against the accidental losses to which they will be exposed. A further guard would be, that one of these copies be on the cuticular membranes of the paper-birch, as less liable to injury from damp than common paper.

The commerce which may be carried on with the people inhabiting the line you will pursue, renders a knowledge of those people important. You will therefore endeavor to make yourself acquainted, as far as a diligent pursuit of your journey shall admit, with the names of the nations and their numbers;

---

3. **heads of the Missouri** the sources of the Missouri River.
4. **fixed by observation** established the position of a place based on measurements or surroundings.

The extent and limits of their possessions;

Their relations with other tribes or nations;

Their language, traditions, monuments;

Their ordinary occupations in agriculture, fishing, hunting, war, arts, and the implements for these;

Their food, clothing, and domestic accommodations;

The diseases prevalent among them, and the remedies they use;

Moral and physical circumstances which distinguish them from the tribes we know;

Peculiarities in their laws, customs, and dispositions;

And articles of commerce they may need or furnish, and to what extent.

And, considering the interest which every nation has in extending and strengthening the authority of reason and justice among the people around them, it will be useful to acquire what knowledge you can of the state of morality, religion, and information among them; as it may better enable those who may endeavor to civilize and instruct them, to adapt their measures to the existing notions and practices of those on whom they are to operate. . . .

In all your [dealings] with the natives, treat them in the most friendly and conciliatory manner which their own conduct will admit; allay all jealousies as to the object of your journey; satisfy them of its innocence; make them acquainted with the position, extent, character, peaceable and commercial dispositions[5] of the United States; of our wish to be neighborly, friendly, and useful to them, and of our dispositions to a commercial [relationship] with them; confer with them on the points most

---

5. **dispositions** (DIS puh ZI shunz) *n.* leanings.

A **memorandum** is often written using the *imperative*, or command, form. In the final paragraph, underline three commands that Jefferson gives Lewis. Circle the verb in each example.

convenient as mutual emporiums,[6] and the articles of most desirable interchange for them and us. If a few of their influential chiefs, within practicable distance, wish to visit us, arrange such a visit with them, and furnish them with authority to call on our officers on their entering the United States, to have them conveyed to this place at the public expense. If any of them should wish to have some of their young people brought up with us, and taught such arts as may be useful to them, we will receive, instruct, and take care of them. Such a mission, whether of influential chiefs, or of young people, would give some security to your own party. Carry with you some matter of the kine-pox; inform those of them with whom you may be of its efficacy as a preservative from the small-pox, and instruct and encourage them in the use of it. This may be especially done wherever you winter.

10

10

11

---

6. **emporiums** (em POR ee ums) *n.* trading centers.

Check Your Comprehension

1. What information does Jefferson consider so important that he wants Lewis to make multiple copies of it?

   _____

   _____

2. How is Lewis to treat the Native Americans he meets?

   _____

   _____

Applying the Reading Strategy

Analyzing Text Structures: Patterns of Organization

3. Which pattern of organization—chronological order, order of importance, or enumeration—is **not** used in the memorandum?

   _____

4. Listed below are four actions that Jefferson asks Lewis to take in the memorandum. Using the numbers 1 through 4, put the actions in chronological order.

   ____ Make several copies of your notes.

   ____ Treat the native people in a friendly way.

   ____ Record your observations about latitude and longitude.

   ____ Meet and learn about the native people.

Writing Informational Materials

   On a separate sheet of paper, write a short memorandum reminding your fellow students of an upcoming school event. Before the body of the memorandum, present a heading with the following lines:

To:
From:
Date:
Subject:

About Public Documents

Public documents relate to laws and issues that concern all citizens. For this reason, these documents are made available for all citizens to read, analyze, and discuss.

This public document is one of the most important in United States history. It is the text of a formal announcement that President Abraham Lincoln signed on January 1, 1863, calling for the freeing of "all persons held as slaves" within the rebellious southern states. Many historians believe that this public document altered the nature of the Civil War.

Reading Strategy

Analyzing an Author's Beliefs

Some public documents, such as census reports, are almost completely objective; they merely record information without supporting a particular point of view.

When public documents contain opinions, however, you must read critically to **analyze an author's beliefs**. To do so, identify the writer's opinions and consider the beliefs and assumptions that support these ideas. Keep these points in mind:

- Writers can state assumptions *explicitly*, telling you exactly what they think.
- More often, writers make *implicit* assumptions. As a reader, you must note what general ideas must be true for the arguments to be true.

Analyzing an Author's Beliefs

Step one

Look for opinion words such as *I think, I believe,* or *in my opinion,* which signal explicit beliefs.

Step two

Look for other words that suggest implicit opinion. These may be adjectives that have clear opposites. For example, a writer might say that a course of action is *just;* another might say it is *unfair.*

Step three

Look for details that suggest a specific point of view. Read the document sentence by sentence. Consider whether each detail is factual or whether someone could make an argument against it.

BUILD UNDERSTANDING

Knowing these words will help you read this public document.

emancipation (ee MAN suh PAY shuhn) *n.* setting free of people from slavery

proclamation (PRAHK luh MAY shuhn) *n.* something that is announced officially

rebellion (rih BEL yun) *n.* a state of armed resistance to one's government

By the President of the United States of America:

A Proclamation.

1   Whereas, on the twenty-second day of September, in the year of our Lord one thousand eight hundred and sixty-two, a proclamation was issued by the President of the United States, containing, among
5   other things, the following, to wit:

"That on the first day of January, in the year of our Lord one thousand eight hundred and sixty-three, all persons held as slaves within any State or designated part of a State, the people whereof shall then be in
10   rebellion against the United States, shall be then, thenceforward, and forever free; and the Executive Government of the United States, including the military and naval authority thereof, will recognize and maintain the freedom of such persons, and will do no act or acts to repress such persons, or any of them, in
15   any efforts they may make for their actual freedom"

"That the Executive will, on the first day of January aforesaid, by proclamation, designate the States and parts of States, if any, in which the people thereof, respectively, shall then be in rebellion against the
20   United States; and the fact that any State, or the people thereof, shall on that day be, in good faith, represented in the Congress of the United States by members chosen thereto at elections wherein a
25   majority of the qualified voters of such State shall have participated, shall, in the absence of strong countervailing testimony, be deemed conclusive evidence that such State, and the people thereof, are not then in rebellion against the United States."

© Pearson Education, Inc.   Reading Informational Materials: Public Documents **223**

◆ Reading Public Documents

The source and type of a **public document** is usually presented clearly. Who is the source of this document?

_____

What type of document is it?

_____

◆ Read Fluently

Many public documents are written in language that provides a great amount of detail. Read the bracketed paragraph aloud. Then, find three details in the paragraph to answer the following questions:

1. Whom does this proclamation affect?

_____

2. How will these people be affected?

_____

3. Who must recognize the effect of the proclamation?

_____

_____

_____

◆ Reading Strategy

One way to **analyze an author's beliefs** is to look for words that suggest an opinion. Look at the underlined passage. What belief about war do Lincoln's words express?

_____

_____

_____

◆ Stop to Reflect

Proclamations often contain legal and formal language. Underline three examples of such language in the bracketed paragraph. Why do you think such language is used?

_____

_____

_____

Now, therefore I, Abraham Lincoln, President of the United States, by virtue of the power in me vested as Commander-in-Chief, of the Army and Navy of the United States in time of actual armed rebellion against the authority and government of the United States, and as a fit and necessary war measure for suppressing said rebellion, do, on this first day of January, in the year of our Lord one thousand eight hundred and sixty-three, and in accordance with my purpose so to do publicly proclaimed for the full period of one hundred days, from the day first above mentioned, order and designate as the States and parts of States wherein the people thereof respectively, are this day in rebellion against the United States, the following, to wit:

Arkansas, Texas, Louisiana, (except the Parishes of St. Bernard, Plaquemines, Jefferson, St. John, St. Charles, St. James Ascension, Assumption, Terrebonne, Lafourche, St. Mary, St. Martin, and Orleans, including the City of New Orleans) Mississippi, Alabama, Florida, Georgia, South Carolina, North Carolina, and Virginia, (except the forty-eight counties designated as West Virginia, and also the counties of Berkley, Accomac, Northampton, Elizabeth City, York, Princess Ann, and Norfolk, including the cities of Norfolk and Portsmouth[)], and which excepted parts, are for the present, left precisely as if this proclamation were not issued.

And by virtue of the power, and for the purpose aforesaid, I do order and declare that all persons held as slaves within said designated States, and parts of States, are, and henceforward shall be free; and that the Executive government of the United States, including the military and naval authorities thereof, will recognize and maintain the freedom of said persons.

35

40

45

50

55

60

65   And I hereby enjoin upon the people so declared to be free to abstain from all violence, unless in necessary self-defence; and I recommend to them that, in all cases when allowed, they labor faithfully for reasonable wages.

70   And I further declare and make known, that such persons of suitable condition, will be received into the armed service of the United States to garrison forts, positions, stations, and other places, and to man vessels of all sorts in said service.

75   And upon this act, sincerely believed to be an act of justice, warranted by the Constitution, upon military necessity, I invoke the considerate judgment of mankind, and the gracious favor of Almighty God.

In witness whereof, I have hereunto set my hand and
80 caused the seal of the United States to be affixed.

Done at the City of Washington, this first day of January, in the year of our Lord one thousand eight hundred and sixty three, and of the Independence of the United States of America the eighty-seventh.

85 By the President: *Abraham Lincoln*
Secretary of State.   *William H. Seward*

◆ **Reading Strategy**

What **belief** is explicitly stated by Lincoln in the bracketed paragraph?

_____
_____
_____

Reading Informational Materials

Place and date are key elements of a **public document**. When and where was the Emancipation Proclamation written?

_____
_____

Why do you think this information is important?

_____
_____
_____

Check Your Comprehension

1. According to Lincoln, why does he have the authority to make this proclamation?

_____

2. Which parts of the United States that practiced slavery are not included in the proclamation?

_____

Applying the Reading Strategy

Analyzing an Author's Beliefs

3. Identify Lincoln's explicit and implicit beliefs in the Emancipation Proclamation. Note beliefs about

the Constitution's authority: _____

_____

the necessity of emancipation: _____

_____

God's existence: _____

_____

Writing Informational Materials

Choose one of the paragraphs in the Emancipation Proclamation. Jot down the key elements of the paragraph. Then, rewrite the paragraph in your own words. Attach another sheet of paper if you need more room.

_____

_____

_____

_____

_____

READING INFORMATIONAL MATERIALS

About Public Relations Documents

A **public relations document** presents the public face of a company or organization. Some familiar public relations documents are advertisements and press releases. Less familiar, but equally important, are mission statements. These statements reveal the mission, or purpose, of a business or organization by presenting three kinds of information:

1. "Who We Are"—a description of the purpose of the organization or business
2. "What We Do"—details that describe services or products
3. "Why We Do It"—a summary of an organization's philosophy and goals

Read the mission statement and calendar of events from the Museum of Afro-American History. As you read, think about how the museum's mission is carried out through the types of events it sponsors.

Reading Strategy

Making Inferences

Inferences are assumptions that you make when reading. When information is not directly stated in a text, alert readers draw on previous knowledge to fill in gaps. As you read, make inferences, then constantly test these inferences by reading further in the text. If further reading casts doubt on your inferences, revise them or form new ones.

Look for Details		Relate Your Experience		Make and Check an Inference
In an article about a fire, notice details about the intensity of the blaze.	+	Recall fires that you have seen.	=	Both skill and courage played a part in putting out the fire. Check against firefighters' actions. Verify.

BUILD UNDERSTANDING

Knowing this word will help you read these public relations documents.

artifacts (ART uh FAKTS) *n.* man-made objects that survive from earlier historical periods

Mission Statement

A Foundation for the Future

The mission of the Museum of Afro-American History is to preserve, conserve and interpret the contributions of people of African descent and those who have found common cause with them in the struggle for liberty, dignity, and justice for all Americans. Therefore, we:

- collect and exhibit artifacts of distinction in this field and acquire and maintain physical structures and sites through the end of the 19th century;
- educate the public about the importance of the Afro-American historical legacy in general, its Boston and New England heritages, in particular;
- celebrate the enduring vitality[1] of African American culture;
- and advance on our own and in collaboration with others an appreciation of the past for the benefit of the custodians of the future.

1. **vitality** (vī TAL uh tee) *n.* power and endurance.

MUSEUM OF AFRO-AMERICAN HISTORY BOSTON
Calendar of Events

Events take place at 8 Smith Court, Beacon Hill, unless otherwise noted.

SATURDAY, FEB. 3, 7:30 P.M.

20 READING AND BOOK SIGNING

On Her Own Ground: The Life and Times of Madam C.J. Walker[2]

A'Lelia Bundles, former deputy bureau chief of
ABC News in Washington and great-great grand-
25 daughter of Madam C.J. Walker, will discuss the
writing of *On Her Own Ground*, the first historically
accurate account of this legendary entrepreneur
and social activist.

Sponsored by the Collection of African American
30 Literature, a partnership between the Museum of
Afro-American History, Suffolk University, and
Boston African American Historic Site.

REFRESHMENTS AND BOOK SALES FOLLOWING. FREE

TUESDAYS, 10:30–11:30 A.M.

35 ### Stories from African American Literature and Lore

Vibrant stories and activities presenting history for
preschool aged children and parents. FREE

2. **Madame C.J. Walker** (1867–1919) an African American woman who
started her own beauty products company geared to the needs of African
Americans. Praised as "the first black woman millionaire," Walker donated
freely to charities and social causes.

◆ Reading Strategy

Read the description of
the first event. Do you
think Ms. Bundles's
portrayal of C.J. Walker
would be positive?

_____

What clues from the text
and from previous
experience allow you to
make that **inference**?

_____

_____

_____

How could you check
your inference?

_____

_____

◆ Stop to Reflect

How well does the Underground Railroad event fit the mission of the museum? Explain.

_____

_____

_____

_____

Reading Informational Materials

A **calendar of events** provides the public with basic information about upcoming events. Circle the dates, times, and admission fees for the Underground Railroad and jazz concert events.

FRIDAY, FEB. 16, 6 P.M.–9 A.M.

Museum Overnight: Underground Railroad[3]

Spend the night at the Museum exploring the Underground Railroad through the escape routes on Beacon Hill. Design and build your own safe house. Includes dinner, storytelling, activities, breakfast and a special "bundle" to take home.

GRADE 5-6. $30 NON-MEMBER $25 MEMBERS.

SUNDAY, MARCH 18, 3 P.M.

Marian Anderson/Roland Hayes Concert Series: A New Beginning

Makanda Ken McIntyre Jazz Quartet. Original jazz selections and standard favorites from this world-class composer and improviser.[4] McIntyre, a Boston native and NY resident, is a master of the alto sax, bass clarinet, oboe, flute, and bassoon. Reception immediately following.

Sponsored in part by the Office of Community Collaborations and Program Development at the New England Conservatory.

$10 NON-MEMBER; FREE MEMBER; GROUP RATES AVAILABLE.

---

3. **Underground Railroad** a system of safe houses set up by opponents of slavery before the Civil War. The "railroad" was established to help escaped slaves reach the Free States and Canada.
4. **improviser** (IM pruh VĪZ er) *n.* a musician who composes music on the spot as he or she plays.

Check Your Comprehension

1. **(a)** Summarize the museum's mission.

   _____

   (b) Name two goals that result from that mission.

   _____

2. Review the calendar of events to answer the following questions:

   (a) In what ways does the museum collaborate, or team up, with others?

   _____

   (b) In what ways does the museum educate the public?

   _____

Applying the Reading Strategy
Making Inferences

3. Complete this chart of inferences about the Museum of Afro-American History. Verify each inference by noting a supporting detail from the mission statement or calendar of events.

Inference	Verification
Some African American artists found a creative outlet in New England.	
The museum founders thought that African American history had been misrepresented.	
The museum has little information about the civil rights movement of the 1960s.	

Writing Informational Materials

Write a mission statement for one of the following organizations:
- A museum devoted to a scientific or an artistic topic
- A magazine devoted to a sport or hobby

Before you write, think about the philosophy of the organization. Then, identify the goals that would arise from that philosophy. Jot down your ideas on another sheet of paper. Then, write your mission statement.

About Critical Commentaries

A **critical commentary** is a piece of writing that analyzes and evaluates a work of art, an artistic performance, or a piece of literature.

- Some critical commentaries address the work itself. For example, a critical commentary might discuss the strengths and weaknesses of a novel or a symphony.
- Other critical commentaries use the work as a springboard to a larger discussion. In "On Social Plays," Arthur Miller discusses tragic drama, but then goes on to offer his view of trends in society and contemporary values.

Reading Strategy

Interpreting an Author's Arguments

To gain the most from a critical commentary, **interpret its arguments**—the major points the author makes and the support he or she gives them. To interpret an argument, determine its meaning and importance. Then, share it in terms that others can understand, even if they have not read the work. These strategies can help you interpret an argument:

Determine the Meaning	Share the Meaning
• After you read the commentary, summarize its main point. • Make sure your summary is supported by the text. • List the evidence—examples or other details—the author provides to support his or her view. • Notice how the author's word choice affects the message.	• Rewrite the main point as if you were sharing it with someone who had not read the commentary. • Summarize the author's argument. • Prepare a two-minute talk about the commentary. Explain its meaning and why it is important.

BUILD UNDERSTANDING

Knowing these words will help you read this critical commentary.

social plays dramas that deal with an individual's conflict with society. For example, in many of Arthur Miller's plays, characters are forced to battle with society over their rightful place in it.

integers (IN tuh jerz) *n.* numbers

from *On Social Plays*

Arthur Miller

◆ Reading Critical Commentaries

This **critical commentary** includes long sentences and paragraphs that are dense with meaning. Use the following strategies to help you read this challenging selection:

- Read slowly and look up unfamiliar words in the dictionary.
- Summarize each paragraph as you read.

◆ Read Fluently

Read the first paragraph aloud. Based on what you read and the underlined passage, do you think the world that Miller describes currently exists? Explain.

_____

_____

_____

_____

1   Time is moving; <u>there is a world to make</u>, a civilization to create that will move toward the only goal the humanistic, democratic mind can ever accept with honor. It is a world in which the human being can
5 live as a naturally political, naturally private, naturally engaged person, a world in which once again a true tragic victory may be scored.

    But that victory is not really possible unless the individual is more than theoretically capable of being
10 recognized by the powers that lead society. Specifically, when men live, as they do under any industrialized system, as integers who have no weight, no *person*, excepting as customers, draftees, machine tenders, ideologists, or whatever, it is
15 unlikely (and in my opinion impossible) that a dramatic picture of them can really overcome the public knowledge of their nature in real life. In such a society, be it communistic or capitalistic, man is not tragic,[1] he is pathetic.[2] The tragic figure must have

◆ Reading Critical Commentaries

Mark the Text

    In this **critical commentary**, Miller states his belief that industrial society takes away the individuality of people. Circle several persuasive words in the bracketed section that Miller uses to get this point across.

---

1. . . . **man is not tragic** Miller is comparing modern man to a tragic hero, who faces suffering and failure with courage and dignity.
2. **pathetic** (puh THE tik) *adj.* arousing pity.

certain innate powers which he uses to pass over the boundaries of the known social law—the accepted mores[3] of his people—in order to test and discover necessity. Such a quest implies that the individual who has moved onto that course must be somehow recognized by the law, by the mores, by the powers that design—be they anthropomorphic[4] gods or economic and political laws—as having the worth, the innate value, of a whole people asking a basic question and demanding its answer. We are so atomized[5] socially that no character in a play can conceivably stand as our vanguard,[6] as our heroic questioner.

Our society—and I am speaking of every industrialized society in the world—is so complex, each person being so specialized an integer, that the moment any individual is dramatically characterized and set forth as a hero, our common sense reduces him to the size of a complainer, a misfit. For deep down we no longer believe in the rules of the tragic contest; we no longer believe that some ultimate sense can in fact be made of social causation,[7] or in the possibility that any individual can, by a heroic effort, make sense of it. Thus the man that is driven to question the moral chaos in which we live ends up in our estimate as a possibly commendable but definitely odd fellow, and probably as a compulsively driven neurotic.[8] In place of a social aim which called an all-around excellence—physical, intellectual, and moral—the ultimate good, we have set up a goal which can best be characterized as "happiness"—namely, staying out of trouble.[9] This concept is the end result of the

---

3. **mores** (MOR ayz) *n.* customs; unwritten laws.
4. **anthropomorphic** (AN throh poh MOR fik) *adj.* having human characteristics.
5. **atomized** (AT uh MĪZD) *adj.* broken into small, disconnected pieces.
6. **vanguard** (VAN GAHRD) *n.* leading part of an army or other group.
7. **social causation** social forces.
8. **neurotic** (noo RAH tik) *n.* person suffering from mental or emotional imbalance.
9. **a social aim . . . staying out of trouble** Miller is contrasting the ancient Greek ideal of *areté* (excellence; virtue) with the modern drives for conformity and comfort.

◆ Reading Strategy

In the bracketed section, Miller's **argument** is that modern society has so many different types of people, none can be the basis of a generalization or a character in drama. Why doesn't Miller believe that a dramatic hero can exist in modern society? Underline words and phrases that answer this question.

◆ Reading Check

Read the underlined sentence. Then choose the interpretation that is closest in meaning to the sentence.

_____ People want to be comfortable and stay out of trouble.

_____ Happiness involves striving for excellence.

_____ Most people want to be the best they can be—physically, intellectually, and morally.

truce which all of us have made with society. <u>And a truce implies two enemies.</u> When the truce is broken it means either that the individual has broken out of his ordained[10] place as an integer, or that the society

55 has broken the law by harming him unjustly—that is, it has not left him alone to be a peaceful integer. In the heroic and tragic time the act of questioning the-way-things-are implied that a quest was being carried on to discover an ultimate law or way of life

60 which would yield excellence; in the present time the quest is that of a man made unhappy by rootlessness and, in every important modern play, by a man who is essentially a victim. We have abstracted[11] from the Greek drama its air of doom, its physical destruction

65 of the hero, but its victory escapes us. Thus it has even become difficult to separate in our minds the ideas of the pathetic and of the tragic. And behind this melting of the two lies the overwhelming power of the modern industrial state, the ignorance of each

70 person in it of anything but his own technique as an economic integer, and the elevation of that state to a holy, quite religious sphere.

◆ **Stop to Reflect**

Read the underlined sentence. Who are the two enemies Miller describes?

1. _____

_____

2. _____

_____

Based on this **critical commentary,** what kind of plays would you expect Miller to write?

_____

_____

Reading Informational Materials

In this **critical commentary,** Miller's main point relates to the influence of industrialized society over people, and therefore over literature. Does Miller believe that this influence is good or bad?

_____

Explain.

_____

_____

_____

_____

_____

_____

10. **ordained** (or DAYND) *adj.* assigned; appointed.
11. **abstracted** (ab STRAK tid) *v.* taken; separated.

Check Your Comprehension

1. What does Miller mean when he calls people "integers"?

   _____

2. According to Miller, what must happen before a person can achieve "a true tragic victory" in the world?

   _____

   _____

Applying the Reading Strategy

Interpreting an Author's Arguments

3. Why does Miller disapprove of happiness as a goal?

   _____

   _____

4. Briefly summarize Miller's ideas about industrialized society.

   _____

   _____

   _____

Writing Informational Materials

Think of a story you have read recently. Then choose the statement that most accurately describes your opinion:

- The story is true to life because . . .
- The story is not true to life because . . .

In a brief critical commentary, use the story as a springboard for sharing your views about some aspect of life. Write your commentary on a separate sheet of paper.

VOCABULARY BUILDER

As you read the selections in this book, you will come across many unfamiliar words. Mark these words and look them up in a dictionary. Then use these pages to record the words you want to remember. Write the word, the selection in which it appears, its part of speech, and its definition. Then, use the word in an original sentence that demonstrates its meaning.

Try to use these new words in your writing and speech. Using the words regularly will help you make them part of your everyday vocabulary.

Word: _____ Page: _____

Selection: _____

Part of speech: _____

Definition: _____

_____

Original Sentence: _____

_____

_____

Word: _____ Page: _____

Selection: _____

Part of speech: _____

Definition: _____

_____

Original Sentence: _____

_____

_____

Word:_____ Page: _____

Selection: _____

Part of speech: _____

Definition: _____

_____

Original Sentence: _____

_____

_____

Word:_____ Page: _____

Selection: _____

Part of speech: _____

Definition: _____

_____

Original Sentence: _____

_____

_____

Word:_____ Page: _____

Selection: _____

Part of speech: _____

Definition: _____

_____

Original Sentence: _____

_____

_____

Word:_____ Page: _____

Selection: _____

Part of speech: _____

Definition: _____

_____

Original Sentence: _____

_____

_____

Word:_____ Page: _____

Selection: _____

Part of speech: _____

Definition: _____

_____

Original Sentence: _____

_____

_____

Word:_____ Page: _____

Selection: _____

Part of speech: _____

Definition: _____

_____

Original Sentence: _____

_____

_____

Word:_____ Page: _____

Selection: _____

Part of speech: _____

Definition: _____

_____

Original Sentence: _____

_____

_____

Word:_____ Page: _____

Selection: _____

Part of speech: _____

Definition: _____

_____

Original Sentence: _____

_____

_____

Word:_____ Page: _____

Selection: _____

Part of speech: _____

Definition: _____

_____

Original Sentence: _____

_____

_____

Word: _____ Page: _____

Selection: _____

Part of speech: _____

Definition: _____

_____

Original Sentence: _____

_____

_____

Word: _____ Page: _____

Selection: _____

Part of speech: _____

Definition: _____

_____

Original Sentence: _____

_____

_____

Word: _____ Page: _____

Selection: _____

Part of speech: _____

Definition: _____

_____

Original Sentence: _____

_____

_____

Word:_____ Page: _____

Selection: _____

Part of speech: _____

Definition: _____

_____

Original Sentence: _____

_____

_____

Word:_____ Page: _____

Selection: _____

Part of speech: _____

Definition: _____

_____

Original Sentence: _____

_____

_____

Word:_____ Page: _____

Selection: _____

Part of speech: _____

Definition: _____

_____

Original Sentence: _____

_____

_____

If you run out of room, continue the Vocabulary Builder in your notebook.

Photo and Art Credits